The Elephants' Graveyard

The Elephants' Graveyard

A Guide for Getting and Keeping Your Welfare Entitlements

Joseph K. Waltenbaugh

WALTENBAUGH.NET

The people and events contained in this work are fictional, and they are used figuratively for descriptive and illustrative purposes only. After all, people like that could not possibly exist. Could they?

CONTENTS

Give a man a fish, and you feed him for a day. Teach a man to fish, and he will complain about the working conditions and demand another fish.

— Modern Welfare Proverb

1 WELCOME TO MY WORLD

THE ELEPHANTS' GRAVEYARD

Okay, so you made it. You're in the building, and no one saw you enter it. The waiting room is crowded, but none of the occupants look familiar. Good. The room has a stark, harsh appearance with nothing to soften or lighten the mood. Row after row of industrial-strength vinyl and steel chairs spread out before you. They are filled with drab people with hardened faces. There are more chairs positioned around the perimeter of the room, some of which are also occupied. The girl at the reception desk seems cold and emotionless, but at least she doesn't ask you any embarrassing questions. You take a seat in the corner against the wall and nervously await your turn. You try to relax, but without success. The gloomy interior and the sickening iridescent glow of the fluorescent lights further increase your anxiety. You fear that you might have stumbled into the Elephants' Graveyard.

Now, what can you expect? You have no experience with this kind of thing. What are you supposed to say? The circumstances surrounding the loss of your job are bizarre and complicated, so much so that even you question what happened. Did you quit, or were you fired? Everything is now so muddled and confusing. How is anyone supposed to know? You attempted to explain the situation to the staff at the unemployment claims office, but they classified your job loss as a "quit" and denied your application for benefits. What if you say the wrong thing now? Can you also be denied welfare benefits? If so, what will you do?

Just then, you see her. She sits directly across from you on the opposite side of the room, under a sign that reads 'NO SMOKING.' She appears calm while puffing defiantly on a cigarette. At least seven children run helter-skelter throughout the waiting room, but she seems oblivious to them. You sense that she has some connection to them, even though she makes no attempt to control their behavior.

Too old to be their mother, you surmise. She appears a visual contradiction—dressed like a teen with a shock of dyed red hair, the unkempt mop entirely matted with graying roots. Her skin is tanned but old and lifeless, sagging limply over her skimpy halter top. She is wearing very short shorts with her legs crossed in your direction. You notice something on the inside of her right thigh—a tattooed line of text, aged and discolored but still legible. It's difficult to ignore, and you cannot help but look closer. 'THIS BELONGS TO CAPTAIN BOB,' it reads with a tattooed arrow pointing farther up her thigh toward her groin. Glancing up, you become aware that she has been watching you. She smiles and winks. She has no front teeth.

"Annie!" the beckoning call sounds from a doorway where a woman with a file folder stands waiting. The name echoes throughout the large waiting room, and the tattooed stranger rises slowly. She gathers the children and struts over to the open door, passing close enough for you to catch her scent—a foul stench—which causes you to gag. The woman with the file folder already seems defeated as she motions Annie and the children into the adjoining room. At the doorway, Annie stops momentarily and throws another wink in your direction. Your first assessment of this place was correct. It is the Elephants' Graveyard. Only an elephant could smell that bad.

Now, think for a moment. What does Annie know that you don't? Why is she so calm and collected, while you're a nervous wreck? How does she know exactly what to say and do to get whatever she wants, and where did she get this information? More importantly, where do you get this information? These are very legitimate questions, and you have come to the right place to find the answers.

It has become common parlance to speak of the welfare system as a social safety net, and it was radio talk-show host Rush Limbaugh who first referred to the safety net as a hammock. And that is the primary purpose of this book: to help you claim your rightful place upon the hammock. However, hammocks can be extremely unstable, as anyone who has experienced one can attest. A change in the political winds can set it spinning and leave you flat on your back. Hopefully, this book will provide you with the necessary strategies to maintain that precarious balance, the steadiness you saw demonstrated by Annie as she strutted past you in the waiting room.

The first thing required, however, is to stop fearing the Elephants' Graveyard. After all, if it is such a terrible place, why are all the elephants dying to go there? And if it is filled with nothing but death and old elephant bones, why are all the great white hunters searching for it? I have watched enough old Tarzan and Jungle Jim movies to know that both humans and pachyderms seem desperate to find the place, so it is reasonable to assume that there is something of value there. But where elephants and hunters must rely on instinct and legend to guide them, you are fortunate enough to have this book to aid you in your quest. And when you reach the Elephants' Graveyard and begin to unlock its secrets, I think you will discover that it is a land filled with shade trees, buffets, spare time, and lots of hammocks.

But to embark successfully on a career at the receiving end of welfare, you must first know what is out there and how to claim your rightful share of it. So before you crawl into that hammock, why not take a stroll by the buffet table? I understand that the "S" suffix soup is exceptional.

2 GETTING ALL YOU CAN GET

"S" SUFFIX SOUP

I spent thirty-two years in the Elephants' Graveyard as a professional welfare employee. For many of those years, I performed federal regulatory compliance audits in the Food Stamp Program and the Aid to Families with Dependent Children (AFDC) cash assistance program. (The names of both programs eventually changed, but I will address that in later chapters.) My audit work involved scrutinizing state welfare records and conducting interviews of welfare recipients in their homes. These home visits always proved enlightening, but they also could be tricky. However, when specific ground rules were followed, everything went smoothly.

One of the basic rules was never to place papers or forms of any kind on a client's kitchen table. To do so would result in the documents sticking to the table and being permanently cemented there. If an adhesive manufacturer could identify and patent the peculiar mixture of foodstuffs and bodily fluids that generally accumulate on a welfare client's kitchen table, he could make a fortune. I always made it a point to avoid client kitchen tables entirely by carrying a clipboard on which I did my writing.

Another rule involved the selection of seating arrangements, namely, never sit on anything other than a hard-backed chair. Overstuffed chairs and couches often lacked sufficient seat support, causing you to sink straight down to the floor with your knees drawn up to your chin. There was also the possibility of picking up fleas, bedbugs, or cockroaches from such furniture. But the main rule—the number one rule—was to never, ever, not under any circumstances, eat in a client's house. That is why I was at a loss to explain Joan's thinking when she began dining with the clients she was auditing.

Joan, a colleague of mine, once casually mentioned to the office staff that a client had fed her lunch during one of her food stamp audit interviews. Her disclosure was a mistake because the office immediately erupted in disbelief, and everyone began chiding her for breaking one of the cardinal rules. She, however, defended her actions by stating that the meal had been quite tasty. The client had served soup. Well, for the remainder of the day, that became the topic of discussion: under what circumstances would we eat a meal prepared by a welfare recipient who was being audited? We decided that if it had to occur, it would be preferable in an "S" suffix home.

In my state, food stamps are given suffix designations depending on the household situation. At that time, they received an "X, R, H, or S" suffix, depending on the type of income present in the home. An "X" suffix household referred to one that received only cash assistance, while an "S" suffix was assigned to a household in which the members received no cash assistance at all. The "S" suffix household had some other source of income, such as wages, unemployment compensation, or Social Security benefits. It generally meant a higher standard of living and, therefore, more sanitary living and eating conditions. That is why we concluded that if we were to eat soup in a client's home, it would have to be "S" suffix soup. Never would we touch "X" suffix soup.

Joan took all this good-natured ribbing rather well. What we didn't know, however, was that she had concocted a scheme to prove her point. She then, unbeknownst to any of us, began collecting recipes from the clients. Whenever she visited a client's home as part of a benefits audit, she made sure to obtain at least one recipe. She even included the recipe requirement on her appointment letters to the clients. Of course, the poor welfare recipients did not understand any of this, but they cooperated and complied nonetheless, mostly out of fear. (Would you not produce anything requested by an IRS agent who was auditing your taxes?)

Then, one day, Joan extended an invitation to all of us to come to her house for dinner the following week. It was to be a different kind of theme dinner, but she refused to provide any information regarding the nature of the theme. She stated only that it was to be a surprise. However, when she greeted us at the door dressed in a battered old bathrobe with a cigarette dangling from her mouth, we began to catch on. The scene looked all too familiar. Her house was a mess, and she had invited neighborhood children into her home to run amok, giving it that unmistakable 'welfare recipient' ambiance. Out in her kitchen, she had arranged, on a sticky table, a smorgasbord of foods prepared from all the recipes she had collected over the months. And to our surprise, the food looked delicious.

The food tasted delicious, too. There were so many dishes I had never seen before, all prepared in a style and manner that surprised everyone. The entire experience proved both enlightening and satisfying. We then loaded our plates and moved into the living room, where we sat around the clutter of kids to eat our "S" suffix soup and watch taped reruns of The Jerry Springer Show.

This now brings me to my point. You wouldn't go to a

new restaurant and order something without first looking at the menu. You might think you know what you want, but what if they have something decidedly different—a unique house specialty—a dish made especially for you? Perhaps something as tasty as "S" suffix soup. You will not know unless you ask. And that also applies to welfare.

Never go into the welfare office and tell them precisely what you want. Go in and ask what you can get. Ask to see the welfare menu. If you tell them what you want, that's all you'll get. And unless you ask, you won't get anything more. There are a lot of entitlement programs out there (e.g., cash assistance, food stamps, Medicaid, home heating energy assistance, child care subsidies, housing subsidies, food bank vouchers, clothing vouchers, auto repair allowances, home weatherization, employment and training programs, etc.), and it is difficult to know what is available at any given time; therefore, you must ask to see the entire list of programs for which you qualify. After you learn what is available, you can then demand it. Seek and ye shall find. Ask and ye shall receive. And when it is given to you, ask for more.

Welfare office employees are paid to answer your questions, but they will not always offer unsolicited information. Therefore, you must be prepared to query them about what is available to you. Remember, always ask to see the menu. And feel free to ignore the prices, as you will never be required to pay for any of it.

3 DEVELOPING THE RIGHT ATTITUDE

HIS EXCELLENCY

He used to parade through town wearing a turban and a white jumpsuit with flared legs and a high starched collar. Rhinestones adorned the shoulders and legs of his jumpsuit with a large plastic emerald brooch clipped to his turban, just above his forehead. He carried a silver-capped cane that he would raise to tap the purple pin in salute to any passerby who addressed him by his title, His Excellency. I cannot recall his real name, but the name he preferred, and the name by which everyone knew him, was Montezuma Gandhi, or more correctly, His Excellency Montezuma Tecumseh George Washington Gandhi. You see, Monty—as I used to call him—was the King of the World and the Spiritual Leader of the Children of Chronos, or so he thought.

Let there be no doubt about it; he actually believed himself to be the leader of all mankind. He also bragged about his marriage to Priscilla Presley and claimed to be awaiting a settlement from the Presley estate. This settlement included a large inheritance that was being held up by someone named Pinky Hathaway. He listed his parents as Armadillo and Poinsettia Presley. (Where he came up with these names, I'll never know.) The only real thing about Monty was his mixed bag of delusions—at least they seemed real to us.

I know all about Montezuma Gandhi because I was his caseworker early in my career until we got him certified as totally bananas and qualified him for Social Security Disability and Supplemental Security Income (SSI). But I never entirely freed myself from him because he continued to receive food stamps and Medicaid.

Monty had the annoying habit of dropping by the welfare office and initiating new food stamp applications to "feed the starving of the world," at least that is what he would write on the application forms. Now, this notion is not that far-fetched; liberal Democrats in Congress have been trying the same thing for years. And some of them also believe themselves to be saviors of all mankind—or maybe just the Children of Chronos. Monty's signed applications were always replete with mentions of Pricilla Presley, Armadillo and Poinsettia Presley, Pinky Hathaway, and the impending Presley estate settlement. All of them concluded with the same footnote that read, "And I really mean it!"

The problem with Monty initiating these food stamp applications was that it required a lot of paperwork and man-hours to reject his requests. The minute he placed his signature on the application form, it had to undergo a myriad of bureaucratic procedures and reviews before being rejected. The federal government closely monitors the application process and requires a full accounting of every food stamp application initiated. It didn't matter that Monty was already receiving food stamps; his applications had to be treated like all others and go through the whole lengthy process. And Monty did not do this just once or twice. He did it all the time. Unfortunately, I was often assigned the task of dealing with his fraudulent applications.

The problem became so severe that we had to instruct the clerks in the reception area to stop giving him applications when he dropped by to request them. That policy probably violated about a dozen federal laws and codes because food stamp applications must always be made available upon request. But, by then, it didn't matter. I had fallen so far behind in my work due to the amount of time I wasted rejecting his applications that something had to be done. So we posted a picture of Monty at the receptionist's desk with the directive that he should not be given a food stamp application under any circumstances. And it worked. From then on, I was able to complete the other functions of my job, and Monty was free to focus more on the Children of Chronos. Unfortunately, the starving of the world did not get fed, but then they never do.

Montezuma Gandhi's attitude was something to be reckoned with. Unbeknownst to himself, he had developed the ultimate welfare strategy. Even if he did not believe himself to be the king of the world, he could have had us on our knees just by pretending he did. First, we got him off cash assistance and out of our hair by qualifying him for Social Security Disability and SSI benefits, something that put more money in his pockets. Then we enticed him with numerous other entitlement programs and offered him all sorts of incentives if only he would stop trying to feed the hungry of the world by filling out those damn food stamp applications. However, he never did stop, and we ultimately changed our entire office policy to accommodate his eccentricity.

It's true that the squeaky wheel gets the grease, and in the world of welfare, a demanding, eccentric client gets a larger share of the pie. The meek may inherit the earth, but meekness will not get you any more welfare entitlements or freebies. Scream, cry, threaten, and stomp your feet—these are the strategies that get you more goodies than the next guy. And if you are the most vocal and the one to complain the loudest, or if you can convince them that you are the king of the world, then you will be sure to get everything you want and then some. "And I really mean it!"

4 PROPER WELFARE LEXICON

COYA

I wish I had invented it, but I didn't. Like everyone else, I didn't even know what it meant. But I liked the word, and I used it quite often. I was not alone in this respect. Many others did the same thing, but they did so only within the confines of my hometown.

I was raised in a small town in the northeast. Besides its chili dogs, smelts, fireworks, and Italians, the creation of the word *coya* is about the only other thing for which the town is known. How it started, no one knows, and what it means is even more of a mystery. But its mysterious origins and its lack of definition in no way retarded its popular appeal.

It seemed to reach its height of popularity during my high school years. But like all nuances of culture, it never actually died. The word is still immortalized in spray-painted graffiti on the outside wall of a local hot-dog shop, and I have been told that it is still deeply etched into the desktops of at least eighty percent of the furniture in the high school. It was only the other day, while seated in a local bar, that I observed someone wearing a T-shirt emblazoned with the word 'COYA' in multicolored lettering. "Hey, Tommy," another bar patron called out. "Is that word coming back?" Tommy looked disdainfully at him and replied, "It never left."

Coya is really hard to define. I guess it is more of a verb than a noun. It is most effective when used as an exclamation directed at someone as a put-down. Coya! Back in high school, it was a sure bet to get you thrown out of class. The teacher didn't know what it meant, but it could not have been anything permissible if it was directed at her with such inflection. Coya! It mattered little that the student vocalizing the insult had no idea what it meant, either (if it meant anything at all). He only knew that it was not appropriate language, and he expected to be punished for using it. Coya! The school administration also had no idea what it meant, but they had seen it painted on the side of the hot-dog shop and carved into the classroom desktops alongside other four-lettered words, so they knew they must punish the student for using such inappropriate language. Coya!

The word coya had only one redeeming and endearing quality—it ended in a vowel. In a town that's ninety percent Italian, that was significant because it made the word sound Italian. A cement finisher I know once told me that if you wanted to get ahead in our town, you had to get down on your knees. That may have worked for him, but for most others in town, it only required being Italian or having a vowel at the end of one's name, making it sound Italian. Many a disgruntled non-Italian political candidate learned this fact the hard way. After losing an election, they could be heard bitching and mumbling to themselves. Of course, almost every anti-Italian slur out of their mouths was prefaced with the word coya.

But other than sounding Italian, the word was just downright nasty. In school, it got you punished. Outside of school, it got you beat up. It is the only intrinsically evil word I know. I conjure up visions of Hell where the damned souls spend eternity in perdition, spewing out the word. I cannot help but wonder what would happen if, during some tense nuclear disarmament talks, one of the negotiators got fed up and blurted out "Coya!" at the opposing delegation. I guess we would all be history by morning.

I borrowed from Rush Limbaugh before, and I intend to borrow from him again. He likes to say "words mean things," and, with the exception of the word coya, they do. Many people talk about welfare benefits, but that is something you must never do if you expect to survive in the Elephants' Graveyard. Words do mean things, and they set the agenda, especially when it comes to welfare.

As a recipient of welfare, the first thing you must learn is that the money and services you receive are not benefits; they are entitlements. The term *benefit* implies something given to you as a result of someone else's caring, consideration, and the ability of that person to give. An *entitlement* is something that is rightfully yours, and denying it to you would be immoral, as well as a violation of your constitutional rights. A benefit can be terminated whenever the benefactor has nothing more to give, but an entitlement, well, it can never be taken away.

Every time you refer to your welfare check or food stamps as a benefit, you erode your base and risk your future as a welfare recipient. What is given to you can be taken away. But every time you make reference to your entitlements, you strengthen your position and secure your future. What is rightfully yours can never be taken away. After all, we live in a country that prides itself on preserving the rights of its citizens.

Words do mean things, and they help create an atmosphere and an attitude affecting the way society thinks and functions. Change the way people talk about things, and you can change the way they feel about them and act upon them. Ensure that society sees welfare as an entitlement, and you will never be in danger of losing it. Purge the word *benefit* from your vocabulary, and replace it with *entitlement*. Use the word often and with pride—and make sure everyone else does too. And if they refuse, try this word on them, "Coya!"

5 DECIDING WHERE TO LIVE

LITTLE HOUSE ON THE PRAIRIE

I described Annie in the first chapter, but I will briefly do so again to refresh your memory. Annie was a woman in her mid-to-late fifties when I knew her. Her tangled mass of wild, red hair resembled a witch's fright wig, and she possessed relatively few teeth. This caused her to spit every time she said my name, and, unfortunately, she prefaced every sentence with it. She had many other unsavory characteristics—chain-smoking, a horrible hacking cough, the inability to tell the truth—and she smelled awful. She proved to be my arch-nemesis during my years as a caseworker.

Annie knew all the ins and outs of receiving welfare, having learned them through years of personal experience. She could play the system like a maestro and gave me a baptism under fire, teaching me lessons I never forgot. Early in my career, I foolishly attempted to visit Annie in her home just to check up on her. It proved to be a learning experience as well as a big mistake, one I never made again.

To this day, I do not know how she found a place so

remote, because, even with the written directions she had provided, it took me almost the whole day to locate it. Since I did not know if Annie knew how to use a noun or a verb, I could not be sure I was reading her directions correctly, so I spent hours haphazardly driving around the countryside, totally lost. Eventually, I came to my senses and realized that Annie's directions were about as reliable as any other piece of information she had ever given me, so I went straight to the post office to enlist their help in finding her house.

At the post office, they referred me to the letter carrier for that area, who kept shaking his head and insisting that I did not want to go there, even if he could provide adequate directions, which he doubted he could. Like the Elephants' Graveyard itself, it was one of those places to which you had to be led. However, upon my insistence, he wrote down his best directions and sent me on my way. It then only took an additional hour before I stumbled upon it, purely by accident. This was in the days before GPS navigation systems, although I doubt even a global positioning satellite could have located the place.

At first sight, I knew it to be the place. The mailman's description was right on target: an impassable, eroded dirt driveway leading to a moat of mud that encircled a dilapidated wooden shack—home sweet home. An old metal mailbox nailed to a tree with the name 'Annie' scrawled on one side of it confirmed that I had arrived at my intended destination. Somehow it all seemed to fit. Annie could have lived nowhere else.

I parked my car along the side of the road and began searching for an alternative route to the house. Of course, I found none and was eventually forced to trudge up the driveway. Even though it had not rained in days, a swamp surrounded the entire shack, and a stream of water trickled from the house down to the road. It was as if the house sat on a natural spring, and it remains a mystery why it did not sink into the murky depths surrounding it. Possibly it was Annie's own stubbornness that kept it afloat—or maybe it was her repulsiveness. Even the creatures in the Black Lagoon did not want her down there with them. But regardless, there it sat, and I had to find a way into it.

When starting out that morning, I had donned my favorite footwear, a pair of tan pigskin western boots. Standing on Annie's front porch, I glanced down to see them covered with mud, almost to the top of the shaft. I think it was then that I fully recognized that I genuinely disliked my job. Up until then, the clients had only insulted my sensibilities and intelligence, but Annie had just insulted my boots, and that was not a wise thing to do.

However, regardless of how upset I was about the boots, my annoyance was no match for Annie's defenses. When she finally let me in, I came face-to-face with her first line of defense—the grandchildren. Of course, they just happened to be visiting along with a whole slew of other relatives. There were no cars anywhere, and no transportation was available for miles, but they were "just visiting." The children immediately started playing with my briefcase, crawling into my lap, writing on my forms, and tossing around the mud they scraped off my boots. But I refused to be intimidated.

Annie perceived my resolve and called upon her next line of defense—the animal world. Like most other clients, Annie shared her abode with a menagerie of dogs. Two of them were pit bulls that wandered into the room on cue and assumed sentry positions on either side of me as I sat at her kitchen table. I had always had an excellent rapport with dogs, so I reached down and petted both of them on their heads before returning to my interview. The memory of my boots still burned, and I was not about to be intimidated or shaken by a couple of canines.

Annie then slid her chair closer to me in a last-ditch effort to drive me out. *The Smell*, I thought. She is trying to use *The*

Smell against me! I countered this tactic by mainly breathing through my mouth to avoid the toxic scent of her unbathed flesh. But then, *The Smell* ceased to bother me as I made an unwelcome discovery that commanded my full attention.

When I had first walked into the shabby cottage, I had been accosted by a few flies. As time progressed, however, so did their annoyance. The other distractions in Annie's home had prevented me from carefully observing the surroundings in the kitchen. When I finally did so, I noticed that flies were everywhere. That revealed two things: 1) somewhere in the house, there was a tremendous amount of rotting food; and 2) if there were that many flies, there had to be even more maggots present.

Like I said, the flies were everywhere, and I mean everywhere. They were all over the counters, all over the table, and all over me. Annie and the others appeared immune to them. I was the only one they seemed to bother, and they kept alighting on my face with ever-increasing frequency. While I wrote, I was forced to shoo them away with my free hand; however, my free hand was mainly engaged in pushing the grandchildren away from my briefcase. It was almost as if the flies had never before encountered the smell of soap and deodorant, and my personal hygiene seemed to attract them like ... well ... like flies! Not once did I see a fly land on Annie or her relatives, and I became reluctant to open my mouth for fear the insects would fly in and gag me.

Finally, I caved. She had won. That was okay with me. I would get my boots cleaned, and everything would be fine, as long as I never had to set foot in that hellhole again. Although I offered no explanation, Annie understood completely. She had won enough times in the past to know when the contest had ended. As I stood and began jamming the papers back into my briefcase, she graciously assisted me. At the time, I did not understand the rule against placing paper forms on a client's kitchen table, so I was forced to leave a few of them behind.

But like any staged event, all agitation was suspended when it became clear that I intended to leave. The actors, all knowing their parts and cues, ceased their annoyances and quickly cleared a path to the door. Even the flies seemed to relent as I turned to leave. I made my escape and never went back.

Annie was many things, but mostly she was a master at warding off unwanted intrusions by nosy auditors and overzealous caseworkers. She did this mainly through the use of the standard client defense mechanisms: repugnant body odor, obnoxious children, and intimidating canines. But Annie also understood that much of it had to do with where you made your home. She insulated herself by becoming inaccessible. That allowed her to set the agenda when dealing with the welfare office. When she wanted or needed something, she would show up and make a nuisance of herself until she received it. When she did not want to be bothered, she kept a low profile, and you did not seek her out. Even if you wanted to find her, you probably couldn't, and that is just how Annie wanted it.

When choosing a home, do not be concerned with trivial things, such as access to public transportation, indoor plumbing, and running water. Think location, and aim for something as remote and inaccessible as possible. If you hope to have a long career on welfare, you will need plenty of privacy. So remember and never forget Annie and her little house on the prairie. I know I never will.

6 LESSONS FROM THE NATURAL WORLD

ARTHUR

It's difficult to write about a friend and effectively communicate all the emotion one feels toward that friend. That's why I've never written about Arthur. Often, in the past, I tried, but my attempts always fell short of what I genuinely wanted to say, so I ended up discarding my writings. This time, however, I think I can do it. And I think I can do it now because I've finally found something to which I can tangibly relate it. I spent five years living with Arthur and learning from him, but it's been thirty-three years since he died, and I find it amazing that he's still teaching me. I should first point out that Arthur was my dog.

From the outset, Arthur fully embraced his role as a member of the canine world. He performed three functions in life: he ate, he slept, and he reproduced. As a young dog and a fraternity mascot, he also drank beer, but he gave up the bottle upon discovering his ability to reproduce. Even Arthur realized that one vice was enough. He was a medium-sized mongrel hound. The hound in him was evident in his bellowing, bugle-like bark and his hound dog features. He preferred to sleep most of the time, at least until he caught wind of a female in heat.

I freely admit it now that I envied him his lifestyle, especially his ability to find other dogs equally willing to reproduce. What can I say? He was a true stud! He succeeded in teaching me how to approach a squirrel undetected, but I could never learn his secret for attracting females or getting a date on Saturday night. Maybe that's because he was never around to teach me that skill. When a female came into heat anywhere within a five-mile radius, he was gone. Sometimes he would be missing for a week or more, after which he would stumble home and sleep for three days straight. He never spoke of his conquests, and since I could not observe him in action, like I could his stalking of squirrels, I never learned his amorous secrets. As a result, all I could do was envy him.

I never asked myself why I continued feeding him, or what contributions he made to the betterment of mankind — or the betterment of me, for that matter. No, I just fed and cared for him, and he took all I had to offer and went his own way. In that respect, he was more like a cat. It never occurred to me not to feed him, and the idea seems absurd even now. Of course, you feed him. You also bathe him and care for him. And, most importantly, you make no demands on him, seeking something in return. By his inherent nature, he gives back to you all he has to offer. He licks your hand and face when you approach him, and he keeps you company when you're alone. He is happy to see you when no one else is, and he teaches your children about the importance of loyalty and love. Additionally, he will forfeit his life in an effort to defend you. He is a dog, and he will make demands of you and take whatever you're willing to offer him. You, on the other hand, need to understand that what he gives in return is worth every sacrifice you make.

Through my work, I had the opportunity to observe the

human side of Arthur, as reflected in some of my clients. Unfortunately, Arthur's lifestyle choices and related activities were not as acceptable when manifested in the lives of the men and women of my caseload. Sleeping eighteen hours a day and demanding food and/or sex for the remaining six hours might be okay for a hound dog, but it did not seem appropriate behavior for human adults. Likewise, requiring others to support you in exchange for nothing, not even a feigned offer of something, is an attitude that is foreign even in the dog world. Arthur had learned the disadvantages of liquor, but it seemed that some of my hardened clients were not that smart.

It struck me that what I found so natural in my dog, I found so objectionable in many of the people I was forced to babysit. Don't get me wrong; I'm not talking about the people who were using the welfare system for its intended purpose. I'm referring to the professional welfare clients who had made careers out of exploiting the system, those who had even less motivation than Arthur.

Maybe it is unfair to equate Arthur with the subculture of serial welfare abusers. After all, Arthur gave me everything a dog could offer. I sometimes think he bestowed on me more than I ever gave him in return, but that is something I'll never know for sure. Perhaps I am too sentimental when reflecting on Arthur and his behavior. The real question is whether society will exhibit the same degree of sympathy and understanding toward the welfare abusers if and when it ever gets around to dealing with them. The ruling class in the Elephants' Graveyard talks a mean game, but it rarely follows through with any meaningful action.

Oftentimes, I would scold Arthur, especially when he would return after having vanished for a long string of days. I would yell at him and threaten to revoke his meal ticket if he did not straighten up and toe the line. He would then look at me with those sad eyes and start licking my face. Of course, I would melt and not carry through with my threats. Naturally, he would not mend his ways and continue as before.

Welfare clients regularly employ similar strategies against their caseworkers, and their maneuvers often prove successful. However, when they tried them with me, they never seemed to work. Tactics that would turn me to butter when employed by Arthur always seemed to turn me to stone when attempted by my clients. Some might label it a lack of compassion on my part, but, as Arthur would tell you, I am only a sucker for a cold, wet nose.

Arthur and all God's creatures can be viewed as role models for anyone in the Elephants' Graveyard who wants to maintain residence there without raising the ire of the caretakers. You might not have sad eyes and soft, floppy ears, and you might not be cuddly and lovable. Still, if you can at least develop some endearing eccentricity, it might make you more acceptable to the caseworkers and administrators. It may also remove the target from your back, allowing you to swing freely in the hammock.

Like Arthur, you have to find something to give them in return that will keep them at bay, be it amusement at some of your oddities or perhaps a terrific recipe for "S" suffix soup. And if that fails, simply quote them Matthew 6:26 that says, "Behold the birds of the air: they neither sow, nor reap, nor gather into barns; yet your heavenly Father feeds them." Despite his carnal appetites and wayward proclivities, Arthur never went hungry. By playing your cards right, neither will you.

7 SAVORING YOUR FREE TIME

ENDLESS SUMMER

On July 1st, the social services union went on strike. The strike affected personnel in the employment offices, welfare offices, and some employees in the state mental hospitals. But most of all, it affected me. We had struck three years earlier, but it had lasted only a few days, and I remember it more as a picnic than anything else. But this time it was different. This time we meant it. We claimed to be striking, not to benefit ourselves, but rather to help those who were yet to be hired. We may have been deluding ourselves, but it did not matter because a kind of religious zeal consumed us. And as any oppressive regime will tell you, an army of religious zealots is not easily conquered.

The state never expected us to strike. Administration officials counted on greed trumping our righteous ideology, and they assumed we would jump at any enticement offered, regardless of the consequences to new and future employees. But in what we considered a rare moment of character and selflessness, we rose from our desks and marched to the picket lines. The state negotiators were caught flat-footed, and they seemed befuddled about what to do. Character and selflessness—as delusional as they might have been in our case—were beyond their comprehension. We knew that we would win in the end or become martyrs in our attempt, which is the same thing as winning if you genuinely believe in your cause.

But it is not the strike itself that I wish to address; it is what went on during the strike, far away from the picket line. If you are going to strike, there is no better time for it than during the summer season. Winter is the most significant deterrent I can see to labor-management problems due to the inclement conditions and the discomfort endured by those walking the picket line. Summer, however, is a different story altogether. The sunshine and warm temperatures take the sting out of it, making it seem a little less bleak. Needless to say, during the time I was not creating havoc on the picket line, I could be found on a nearby beach.

There is much to be said for leisure. The hot summer sun and the soft, balmy breezes work in concert with the tender grittiness of the sand to touch a welcome chord that often suffers from neglect. It is only when this lonesome chord is played that the negligence is realized, and resolutions are made not to wait so long before touching it again. I lay on the beach sipping cold beer while strumming this chord over and over again. I was on strike, had no steady income, and was quickly on my way to becoming a bum. But those facts did not seem to worry me. Besides, my tan was developing beautifully.

It was at a time when the bronze of my skin made my race indiscernible that I began looking around at my environment. Up until then, I had not paid close attention to the inhabitants of this new world because I had been too busy working on my tan and catching some well-deserved Zs on the beach. But when it became physiologically impossible to get any darker and boredom began to settle in, I finally took notice of those around me. What startled me was the fact that many of those sharing my new lifestyle were familiar to me. And I soon realized that they were not sharing my lifestyle; I was sharing theirs. They were there first. I was the new kid on the block.

When I was working and collecting a paycheck, the failure of my clients to keep their appointments with me, especially during the summer, was a major headache. They always had doctor appointments that caused them to miss their appointments with me, or their children had doctor appointments, or the parents had doctor appointments, or their dogs had doctor appointments. It was only after I threatened to terminate their welfare benefits that they finally showed up. However, that was before the strike.

During the strike, I was on the beach, and they were right there beside me, looking healthier and tanner than I was. One thing was certain, though; they were not missing any welfare appointments. Like me, they were not collecting a steady paycheck, and they didn't care. But then neither did I. I blended right into their world. I traded them beers for cigarettes, joined them in complaining about how the country was being run, and I worked on my tan without a worry in the world.

As is the nature of most strikes, this one finally ended after about a month. I cannot recall whether a majority of the people involved concluded that the strike was worthwhile or not. All I know is that one day I had to abandon my hedonistic lifestyle and return to my desk. Even now, when driving past the beach on my way to work on those hot summer mornings, or when I see some client sunbathing in her backyard, I look back with longing and envy to the strike and my lazy days on the fringe of the Elephants' Graveyard.

So what should you do with all the free time welfare will afford you? That is a difficult question to answer because the possibilities are as numerous as the personalities of those you will encounter in the welfare system itself. The trick, however, is not to do anything that will get you thrown off welfare, such as learning a trade or developing a marketable skill. Instead, you should cultivate interests that help extend your stay and aid you in your dream of permanently remaining in this land of sunshine, hammocks, and entitlements. In other words, hone your leisure skills, meet new people, make new children.

8 UNDERSTANDING FOOD STAMPS

HOW MUCH IS THAT IN DOG MONEY?

It was the evening of my last full day at sea, and the ship was scheduled to dock in Miami the following morning, bringing my dream vacation to a close. Embarking upon the ship seven days earlier, I had been presented with a bottle of Asti Spumante, compliments of my travel agent. The cabin steward had it nicely chilled and waiting for me in my cabin when I arrived the first day. But for one reason or another, I neglected to drink it that day. It then sat there for the remainder of the week undisturbed but always nicely chilled. On the last night of my nautical adventure, I relented and cracked open the bottle in the company of two Canadian girls I had met earlier in the week. We laughed and sipped the wine in their cabin while they packed their suitcases in preparation for the following morning's departure.

Suddenly, Jill stood erect and drew her hands from the clutter of her suitcase. "Look what I found!" she cried gleefully. And there, stretched tightly between her fingers, was a crisp, new Canadian one-hundred-dollar bill. I knew immediately that it could not be mine. She then did what would be expected of any grown adult after having spent an entire week in an environment devoid of pressure and responsibility; she acted like an adolescent and began taunting her Canadian roommate by waving the bill in her face.

I think it was then that it hit me. Had I accidentally spilled the wine—heaven forbid—I would have thought nothing of reaching over and sopping up the mess with the Canadian money. Or had Jill set it afire or ripped it up before my eyes, I would not have flinched or blinked. I gladly would have given it away to anyone without a second thought because, to me, it was not real. It was imprinted with a funny colored ink, and it displayed a picture of someone I did not know and did not care to know. It meant no more to me than the remaining remnants of Mexican and Jamaican money I still carried in my pocket. (I did like the Jamaican money, though; it was pretty.)

As Jill danced around the room with her fake money, I did something I usually don't do while vacationing: I began to think. What Jill held in her hand might as well have been Mexican, Jamaican, or Confederate currency. To me, they all seemed equally unreal and worthless. Of course, except for the Confederate money, you could take the foreign currency to the bank and receive some real U.S. dollars—greenbacks—the lifeblood of every American citizen. But that knowledge did not alter the fact that, in its foreign state and appearance, the odd-looking bill did not seem real.

In the United States, we often think of ourselves as adhering to a single monetary standard, but that is not the case. There is another legal tender that permeates our society. However, not all people avail themselves of it, and some spend their entire lives without ever encountering it. Others, unfortunately, do not know life without it. As I sipped the wine and watched the antics of the girls, I realized that Jill could just as easily have pulled out and held up a one-hundred-dollar booklet of food stamps—a negotiable and legal tender, immediately recognizable to members of a particular subculture yet meaningless to others not acquainted with welfare.

I then came to understand how my welfare clients viewed the food stamps I so conscientiously issued to them each month. They would give them away because they did not seem real. They were not careful about where they put them because they did not seem real. They traded them for cigarettes because they did not seem real. They would leave them behind when they moved because they did not seem real. They continually lost them because they did not seem real. And they would sell them for half their value because they did not seem real. But oh, those greenbacks sure were real! To obtain more food stamps, clients would cheat, lie, and steal without remorse. After all, who was ever punished for lifting a little from the bank while playing Monopoly? In other words, they viewed the food stamps exactly the way I had considered Jill's Canadian one-hundred-dollar bill and my pocket full of Mexican pesos and Jamaican dollars.

Eventually, food stamps in the form of paper food coupons went the way of all dinosaurs, a victim of modernization, and they were replaced with digital transfers of real money via electronic exchange technology. Even the name changed from food stamps to *SNAP benefits* (SNAP being the acronym for Supplemental Nutrition Assistance Program). Still, they retained their Monopoly money image with the recipients of the entitlement. Additionally, they continued to be referred to as food stamps by their users in the real world.

The mistake of viewing food stamps as something different—the way I viewed Jill's Canadian money—is a trap into which you must not fall. The secret to surviving in the Elephants' Graveyard is to get as much as you can and not give any of it away. It would be foolish (not to mention illegal) to sell your food stamp benefits (paper or electronic) for a fraction of their value. Would you sell a twenty-dollar bill for ten dollars? I think not. Food stamps are legal tender, and you must treat them as such. You must learn to see beyond their odd appearance and understand what they truly represent—real money.

The world of welfare is like a foreign country. It has its own rules and regulations, and it also has its own currency. Food stamps are its currency, and the only difference between food stamps and U.S. dollars is that food stamps are only redeemable in grocery stores and a few other approved exchange outlets. It is the same as Jill's Canadian one-hundred-dollar bill. To me, it meant nothing, but in Vancouver or Toronto, it bought quite a few TV dinners.

9 AID TO FAMILIES WITH DEPENDENT CHILDREN

PAGAN BABIES

I don't think it is possible to have gone through the Catholic parochial school system in the 1950s and 1960s without having fond memories of the nuns and the values they tried to instill in their students. The Catholic sisters who taught me may have taken a vow of chastity, but that pledge in no way quelled their natural maternal instincts. Those instincts, I believe, were what made them the prime movers behind the yearly campaign known as *Pagan Babies*.

Pagan Babies was an annual drive to raise money for the Christian education of deprived children in poor third-world countries. As school students, we would save our pennies and "purchase" pagan baby stamps that we glued into booklets, much like S&H Green Stamps, which were also popular at the time. After you filled up the required number of books, you "owned" a pagan baby that you got to name. The name was supposedly bestowed upon the child at his or her baptism. The money went to the missions to help defray the costs of educating and supporting these deprived children. Based on the number of pagan babies I have attributed to me, I can only pray that they never come after me for child support.

The Elephants' Graveyard has its own version of pagan babies, and it supports them, not with pennies, but with billions of dollars poured into a program called AFDC. AFDC is an acronym for Aid to Families with Dependent Children, and it means that the federal government will subsidize families with minor children if it can be shown that the children are deprived. Like the Food Stamp Program, which was renamed the Supplemental Nutrition Assistance Program, AFDC was renamed Temporary Assistance for Needy Families, or TANF. Still, I use the name Aid to Families with Dependent Children here because it remains a more descriptive name and a better one for explaining the federal cash assistance program.

A child can be considered deprived and eligible for AFDC if one of the parents living with the child is disabled or has some incapacity. A child can also qualify as deprived if a parent has a sufficient work record and has exhausted all unemployment compensation benefits. But most often, deprivation is established because one or both of the parents is missing from the home due to divorce, separation, abandonment, or anonymity. Usually, it is a deadbeat dad who has flown the coop, but not always.

I say not always because, as a caseworker, I occasionally encountered the unusual situation where the mother was absent from the home. When the mother was reported as deceased and the death could be verified, the absence was entirely legitimate. However, when she was missing for other reasons, the circumstances were always vague, and things never felt right. Horenski was the perfect example of this.

Horenski was his last name, and it was the name by which everyone knew him. I do not know of anyone who called him by his first name, Randall. He received welfare benefits for himself and his son. The boy's mother was absent from the home, and Horenski claimed not to know who she was. In welfare, an unwed mother is required to provide the name of the father, or at least who she thinks the father might be, and the state attempts to establish paternity and collect child support from him. Prior to establishing paternity, the guilty male is referred to as a "putative father."

It is difficult to know how many times I tried to explain to Horenski that the concept of a "putative mother" was impossible. The mother could not have left town before Randall Jr. was born. But Horenski always came back with the same argument: he had been screwing at least five girls back then, and he was not sure which one was the mother. Besides, he was drunk at the time. Unfortunately, Horenski lived in a housing project filled with unwed mothers who kept coaching him on what to say. It did not matter that his assertions made no sense coming from a man, especially Horenski. Logic does not thrive in the Elephants' Graveyard, and it never did. As a matter of fact, it is to be avoided at all costs.

Horenski did say something true. He probably was drunk at the time of his son's conception. That was a safe bet because he was drunk most all of the time. Consequently, he spent a considerable amount of time in jail, which left no one to care for Randall Jr. Fortunately, not only did the women in the housing project provide him with volumes of misinformation about the welfare system, they also looked after his son whenever he took up residence in the drunk tank.

At least three times a year, one of the mothers would march in with Randall Jr. in hand, along with a written statement from his father granting her custody of the boy until Horenski completed his ninety-day tour of the public penal facilities. Horenski would usually scratch out some cryptic message on a piece of notebook paper and have two other inmates witness it. He always liked to get at least one "celebrity" witness. If a big murder or rape trial were taking place, it was a sure bet that the accused would be one of Horenski's witnesses.

Annie, on the other hand, always knew who the father was. That was because she was always married at the time of the child's birth. She had no illegitimate children. She was from the old school of welfare that said, "If you are going to have children, you get married first." The old school said nothing about being married at the time of conception or keeping the old man around after the child was born, but when the kid popped out of the womb, there was always a husband there to catch him. This was one rule she failed to pass along to her daughters, who were busy churning out illegitimate children as if they were contestants in some underground competition or reality show.

Despite her physical appearance, Annie never had a problem scrounging up husbands, which she did at a phenomenal rate. Annie was married more times than anyone I have ever known or even heard of. I had a running contest with another caseworker to see who could name all of Annie's husbands and former surnames. For some reason, I always forgot her fifth husband's name and would inevitably lose the contest.

Almost all of Annie's marriages were typical with predictable outcomes. They mostly followed a similar course before both parties separated, leaving behind a little souvenir bearing the father's name post-scripted with the suffix "Junior." It was these little "bundles of joy" that enabled Annie to stay on the welfare rolls for as long as she wanted, or at least as long as her ovaries continued functioning.

What both Annie and Horenski knew—and what you should also know—is that the surest way to survive in the Elephants' Graveyard is to qualify for AFDC or TANF or whatever name it is going by at the time, and the easiest way to qualify is to have minor children with at least one parent missing. There is always an effort to track down missing parents and squeeze child support out of them for these pagan babies, but it only works if the deadbeats can be found or if they can be identified in the first place. The other option is for one of the parents to be disabled. That allows both parents to live with the children and have a direct hand in their upbringing. Having your spouse or "significant other" around may seem ideal and desirable. It may also be beneficial for the children. But as Annie and Horenski would both argue, it's not as much fun.

10 CHOOSING A DEADBEAT DAD

FATHER GOOSE AND MR. RIGHT

When I was a caseworker, nearly eighty percent of the unwed mothers in my caseload had been impregnated by the same man to give birth to about 220 children. The man's name was Clyde Wooten, but I dubbed him *Father Goose*. All the mothers identified him as the father of their illegitimate children. It was hard to prove differently because he freely admitted fathering all the children, and he gladly would sign an acknowledgment of paternity every time he was asked to do so.

It never failed that when some eighteen-year-old would get pregnant and give birth to a bouncing baby boy or girl, she would walk into the office with a written statement from Clyde claiming responsibility for having fathered the child. Clyde could not leave it at just that, either. He always felt obligated to explain precisely how it had happened. I guess that was part of the price the girls paid for his service. He would rate them in the sack on a scale of one to ten, and he would finish with his usual explanation of how he had blown the end off the condom, and they just don't make them like they used to. I always felt that Clyde could have made a fortune as a test pilot for a prophylactic manufacturer.

But Clyde was not interested in earning any money. At the age of ninety-three, he simply sat back and collected his Social Security and Supplemental Security Income (SSI), which consequently made him immune to any attempts to collect child support from him for all his admitted illegitimate children. He looked exactly like Poopdeck Pappy (Popeye's prodigal father): he was old, unkempt, unshaven, and gruff. He also squinted out of one eye. I always saw him either entering or leaving the Black Whale bar. I think he lived there.

I genuinely believe that when these young girls came to him and asked if he would claim to be the father of their children, he was so flattered that he could not refuse their requests. It was a brilliant scam, and it worked. Having quickly learned the ins and outs of the system myself, I knew the futility of spinning my wheels trying to fight something like this. Instead, I sat back and looked forward to Clyde's next conquest.

I mentioned in the last chapter that Annie was unique in that she liked to marry the fathers and keep them around, at least for a little while. Her idea of the ultimate deadbeat dad was someone with a physical or mental disorder who could not support the children and who would not jeopardize her receipt of welfare by his presence in the home. Like I mentioned earlier, Annie did not stay married long, and the dads did not hang around too long either. However, one marriage managed to last slightly longer than any of the others, and it involved the man whose name I have always had problems remembering.

The reason for my memory lapse is that the guy had two names. He received welfare under both names at two different addresses. He was able to pull this off because, as luck would have it, he also had two different caseworkers. Furthermore, he had a wife at each address, and Annie was one of them.

A coworker of mine first became suspicious and pointed out the inconsistencies to me. She had taken over someone else's caseload and decided to conduct home visits to become more familiar with the clients and the area where they lived. Her friendship with me and my constant complaining about Annie had given her some familiarity with Annie's case and her ever-changing marital status. So, the moment she spotted the guy, she recognized him as Annie's current spouse, based on my description of him and a passing observation she had made when he was in the office one day.

His response was that Annie had married his twin brother (who just happened to have a different last name). We checked the birth certificates in the case records, but neither was issued for twins. On several occasions, we scheduled office appointments for both women at the same time, with the requirement that their husbands accompany them. In each instance, one or the other husband would fail to appear and would offer some flimsy excuse. We were at a loss about what to do next. Where both of us knew how to report a crime such as burglary, murder, or rape, we had not the slightest idea how to go about reporting bigamy, even though we knew it to be equally illegal. Finally, we did the only thing we could think of—we turned to Annie.

Annie's response was not what I had expected. She politely listened to my suspicions and my reasoning behind them, and she then matter-of-factly told me that she already knew. She had known for some time. In fact, she and the other woman had met once to compare marriages and discuss the entire situation. The outcome of this powwow was that both parties were satisfied with the arrangement. In a strange sort of way, they liked it. He spent about two nights with each one and was out of their hair for the remainder of the week. This also led them to conclude that there might be a third wife involved. Annie told me that she felt sorry for the guy. He was not the same since they removed part of his brain. (I was convinced it was the front part.) Besides, he was not hurting anyone, and he seemed to be enjoying himself.

Annie's perspective quickly changed when I told her that we could not allow this to continue. She could stay married to him if she wished. That was fine. I would not report it to anyone (as if I knew whom to report it to), but he could not continue receiving welfare benefits at both houses. Since the other woman had married him first, that is where his share of the money would go. Well, that seemed to make a difference to my old girlfriend. What is the point in having a squeeze around if he only has half a brain, and you don't receive any money for him? I had barely finished informing her of the new rules when she turned around and notified me of their pending divorce. Some things never change.

Odd as it seems, when I look back and think about Annie and what's-his-name, I realize that Annie's marriage to him was about the only one that even had the slightest chance of remaining solvent. And home-wrecker that I was, I had to go and screw it up.

The lesson to be learned from all this is to consider carefully who you choose as a mate if you wish to make your home in the Elephants' Graveyard. What your mother told you about picking a solid husband with strong earning potential doesn't apply here. As a matter of fact, just the opposite is true. What you actually need is someone unknown, untraceable, and unemployed. Oh yes, it also helps if he is physically or mentally deficient in some way. And based on my observations last week during a visit to a shopping mall, I would say that your chances of finding Mr. Right couldn't be better.

11 MEDICAID

IS THERE A DOCTOR IN THE HOUSE?

When I first began working as a caseworker in the Elephants' Graveyard, Medicaid was mainly an afterthought. Training for the caseworker's job involved six months of intense study in a large classroom housed appropriately at one of the state mental institutions. The classroom instruction was supplemented with some on-the-job training experience at the welfare office for a few weeks. Although the training course was particularly intense and comprehensive, it only covered the areas of cash assistance and food stamps. We completed three months of cash assistance instruction and three months of food stamp instruction before returning to the welfare office as full-fledged caseworkers to face Annie and her cronies. Nowhere in the formal training was the subject of Medicaid even raised.

Back then, Medicaid was viewed primarily as something tacked onto the receipt of cash assistance. If you received cash assistance, you automatically qualified for Medicaid—

the blue card. If you did not receive cash assistance, you had to apply for Medicaid—the green card. But when I returned from training and began treading the soil of the Elephants' Graveyard, I did not know how to make Medicaid eligibility determinations. It was not until I had completed a whole month on the job that someone sat me down and, over the course of one afternoon, taught me everything I needed to know about Medicaid. It had taken me six months in the loony bin to learn about cash assistance and food stamps, but, in one afternoon, all the salient points regarding the Medicaid program were explained to me.

I cannot say I grasped everything that was presented to me that day, but I did comprehend the fundamentals: 1) the blue card covered doctor visits, hospital stays, and prescription drugs; 2) the green card covered only doctor visits and hospital stays; 3) people who qualified for cash assistance got the blue card; 4) people who did not qualify for cash assistance got the green card. Armed with that knowledge, I spent the next five years determining people's eligibility for blue and green cards. And that is how we referred to them—blue and green cards—because the Medicaid cards looked identical except for the background and ink colors. It was a straightforward system, easy to understand and manage.

The simplicity of the system foretold its downfall because nothing simple can survive long in the Elephants' Graveyard. Somewhere along the way, Medicaid underwent an expansion of biblical proportions. I am not joking here. The program went from two categories—blue card and green card—to over fifty different categories with 475 subcategories, based on varying circumstances and qualifying aspects. Even people living in the same family were categorized differently to the extent that it became almost impossible to determine who qualified for what, and maybe that was the plan all along. Fortunately, it occurred after I had left the local welfare office and had been promoted to a position where I was no longer directly involved with the Medicaid program.

Shortly after the Medicaid expansion, automation swept through the Department of Public Welfare. Department officials contracted independent technology experts to automate the eligibility determinations and benefit calculations for the cash assistance and food stamp programs, thereby eliminating the human error factor. Despite some setbacks, the programmers managed to achieve their goal; however, when they took their first look at Medicaid, after having been asked to work their magic on that entitlement program as well, they almost fainted. After months and months of careful examination, they concluded that it couldn't be done. Computer systems require some degree of logic, and they determined that the Medicaid program was totally devoid of logic. And since it was impossible to change the laws of causality and mathematics, the programmers informed the caretakers of the Elephants' Graveyard that the only option would be to change the rules of Medicaid.

Since I was never heavily involved with Medicaid after my promotion, I'm not sure what changes they made to the program. However, they managed to make it fit the computer logic well enough to claim they had automated it, although I'm still not convinced they succeeded. Regardless, continued existence in the Elephants' Graveyard means that you will have to deal with the confusion surrounding Medicaid and the attempt to automate it, irrespective of whether or not the automation works. The good part is that you now have a plethora of category slots to choose from to qualify for Medicaid. Even if your medical complaint is only a paper cut or toenail fungus, there is probably a Medicaid category that fits your particular ailment. And if there is not one, just fake it. No one understands the Medicaid program anymore, so no one can tell you with any certainty that you do not qualify. And if you sense frustration and confusion on the part of your caseworker over the entire Medicaid issue and want to further her anxiety, just ask her for the blue card.

12 SURVIVING WORKFARE

LARD ASS

The generic term "workfare" is a play on the words "welfare" and "work," but the official title in my state was the Work Experience Program, which became known primarily by its acronym, WEP (pronounced "weep"). What it meant was that welfare clients were required to work for their welfare checks—no work, no money. Wow, what an idea! For the longest time, I couldn't figure out why someone hadn't thought of it before. However, when I saw them attempt to implement it, I finally understood. The idea had been considered before, but it had never been attempted because it fundamentally does not work.

Besides workfare, there is another common word that describes this type of forced labor. That word is slavery. This country learned long ago that you cannot make people work when their only rewards are continued squalor and hopelessness. Remember the Emancipation Proclamation and the Civil War? Unfortunately, some people have to learn that lesson the hard way, and those who conceived the

Workfare Program fall into that category.

One of the significant problems with the Workfare Program was a flaw in the logic underlying its formulation. The forefathers of welfare erroneously assumed that people want off welfare in order to become productive citizens. Taking it a step further, they also reasoned that welfare recipients would welcome the opportunity to work and repay society for what they had received. But what they did not realize is that most recipients do not consider their receipt of welfare as a debt incurred against society. They see it as a right and a debt owed to them by society. So they grab as much as they can for as long as they can. In other words, what the creators of the workfare concept did not count on were the likes of Lard Ass.

Lard Ass was the first person I called into the office to enroll in the Workfare Program. At the time, I was still a rookie caseworker and somewhat naïve. I was also extremely excited about the Workfare Program and all it represented. Lard Ass, however, was not as impressionable as I was, and he certainly was not one to get excited over something as mundane as a new welfare program, especially one that had the word "work" as part of its name.

I should point out that Lard Ass was Annie's son. His age was somewhere in the early to mid twenties, and I don't think he had ever held a job in his life. Except for a few brief and unsuccessful excursions into the real world, he had lived with his mother since birth and continued to do so. Having passed the age of twenty-one, he was able to receive state-funded welfare benefits on his own for a set number of days every year. When his period of eligibility would end, he would have himself added back onto his mother's federally funded welfare case. It was all legal and quite common at the time. Annie had taught him well, and he was familiar with most of the loopholes in the welfare system.

Unwashed and unshaven, Lard Ass sat before me, clothed in an old, beat-up pair of jeans, a sleeveless T-shirt, and, of course, his tattoos. Each forearm had one, both self-inflicted with a blue fountain pen. One spelled out the name *JANE* (naturally, the "N" was written backward). Evidently, Jane had been a former girlfriend and someone with whom he had fathered an illegitimate child. The other tattoo simply read *MOM*. Of this one, Annie was particularly proud.

He also had tattoos on each hand. These had been branded onto him by someone with a bit more tattoo experience, and they looked more professional and legible. Like those on his arms, they were simply letters and punctuation spelling out a message. One was inscribed on each finger at the base near the knuckle. When Lard Ass would extend his fists and place them side-by-side, the meaning was clear to anyone standing opposite him. The message read *F-U-C-K Y-O-U-!*.

That pretty much says all there needs to be said about Lard Ass, except perhaps for his name. According to his birth certificate, *Lardass* was his legal name. It was the one Annie had given him at birth, but he went by the name Lars instead. Annie even called him Lars, as did most everyone else. But I always called him Lard Ass—and I pronounced it *LARD-ASS*—because I found the name hilarious, and also because it was his legal given name. I could not bring myself to call him Lars. For me, the name Lars invokes the image of a Scandinavian youth: tall, strong, blonde, and athletic. But looking at Lard Ass with his greasy black hair and spotty goatee, his heavy metal T-shirt and torn jeans, I could not bring myself to call him Lars. No, he was Lard Ass, and I only had to be obscenely insulted once by his knuckles to know that he would always be Lard Ass.

Another quirk of his name was that Annie also called one of their dogs Lard Ass. When this situation got too confusing, she began calling the human Lard Ass "Lars." I maintained that it would have taken the dog less time to adjust to the name change, but, nevertheless, Lard Ass began answering to his new name, and everyone called him Lars from then on—that is, everyone but me.

So there I had Lard Ass with me in the office, one on one, *mano a mano*. Together, we were going to analyze his "barriers to employment" by involving him in a workfare assignment that would lead to permanent, gainful employment. It was to be a joint effort—my guiding hand and his hard work. Poverty did not stand a chance because the dynamic duo had entered the ring, and we were primed and ready to kick some butt, or so I thought.

Lard Ass soon realized that his visit to the office that day was not likely to be a short one, and he came to accept the fact that he was going to have to humor me and offer at least some minimal cooperation. He understood most of the requirements for keeping his welfare benefits, and he knew that cooperating with the employment and training requirement was one of the biggies. Having been thrown off welfare once before and sanctioned for refusing to cooperate with work registration, he had learned a valuable lesson. So he relented and stared blankly at the list of available workfare jobs while I lectured him on the glories of the Workfare Program.

After observing him stare at the list for an unusually long time, I concluded that Lard Ass could not read. There was no need to go any further with my assessment of his employment needs. He could not be enrolled in the Workfare Program or any other employment-related activity until we taught him to read. At first, he was a little reluctant to admit his handicap, but I finally pried it out of him. I explained how we could send him to reading classes. These classes would constitute the total of his work plan until he finished. Then, we would establish a new work plan. He thought for a moment and then nodded his head. Reading class? Yeah, he could handle that.

And so it was that Lard Ass returned to school ten years after having dropped out in the tenth grade. It was not quite school, but rather a literacy class sponsored by the public library; however, it was a start. I was full of hope, and I had already arranged for him to earn his GED (i.e., high school equivalency diploma) upon the completion of his reading classes. That would be followed by some on-the-job training in a workfare job. And then who knows? Lard Ass, on the other hand, had other ideas.

At first, the literacy classes struck him as an easy way out. He had bluffed his way through ten years of public education, so he felt this class would be a walk in the park. It sure beat working, and the classes only met two evenings a week. However, he soon grew bored with the classes as they began encroaching on his nightly social activities, prompting him to employ a time-honored technique he had perfected in his earlier school days—he disrupted the classes until they threw him out and refused to readmit him.

Of course, when I became involved, he denied any wrongdoing. He swore up and down that it was all a conspiracy against him, as everything in his life had been. People kept putting him down, making him stay on welfare. Besides, he had accidentally bumped his head and could now read. It was a miracle! All the rest of those illiterate douchebags in the class were jealous of him, so they made up those lies and had him thrown out. Screw them! He no longer needed their reading course. He then picked up one of the workfare brochures and read it aloud better than I could have done.

As I mentioned earlier, I was highly supportive of this program, and it tended to cloud my judgment and awareness of what was actually happening. I did some stupid things in those early years, but none could compare with the asinine mistakes I made in my effort to ensure the success of the Workfare Program. Back then, I believed in what I was doing and in what the department was doing, so I immediately enrolled Lard Ass in a GED class so he could earn his high school diploma equivalency.

The GED class was much more structured, and it met more often than the reading class, thus cutting further into Lard Ass' social life. The instructor was an old, retired school teacher, and she did not take crap from any of her students. She was on Lard Ass' ass from day one, as she had been on his ass when she had taught him in the third, fourth, and fifth grades. She, unlike the miraculous knock on his head, was probably the reason Lard Ass could read. Needless to say, she scared the Hell out of him—but only in the short term.

All too soon, he came to realize that he was no longer nine years old but an adult with no reason to fear this woman, so he began disrupting her classes as he had done in the reading class until she also threw him out. Like Lard Ass, she realized that she had grown too old to put up with that kind of nonsense. Lard Ass then repeated his claim of no wrongdoing and reverted to his premise of a concerted plot against him. He even went so far as to suggest that the teacher had been the initiator of the conspiracy back when he was in third grade. He had been doomed from the start!

I could not impose any discipline on him because, by the definition of the welfare policy, he was cooperating with me. I could not throw his ass off welfare or suspend his checks and food stamps because he always attended the classes—that is, until he was no longer permitted to do so. The policy did not address the situation where he would plunge the classroom into chaos once he got there, but welfare policy never does address real-life situations. So, I had to come up with something else, and work seemed the only other option. Yeah, work! That will teach him. My liberal social worker attitude had turned into cynicism and a desire to punish and get even with him.

It just so happened that there was a workfare assignment available with the state highway department, so I immediately slotted Lard Ass into it. No more screwing around; he would now be required to work for his welfare check. I told my fellow caseworkers that I hoped the leathernecks on the construction crew would straighten his ass out, but what I anticipated was his quitting the minute the other lard asses sloughed off all their work on him. I could then shut off his benefits and be rid of him for a while.

Whether or not he survived the job, Lard Ass was a lifer on welfare, and I knew that I would always be dealing with him. All I could hope for were brief reprieves when he would screw up, and I could take short vacations from him. It had not taken him long to quell my enthusiasm for workfare or any other employment and training program and awaken me to the reality of the Elephants' Graveyard. Now, all I wanted was revenge.

As with most things I plan, this did not turn out as I had expected. Lard Ass did not quit the job, and I did not get to sanction him. He instead hit one of his coworkers on the head with a shovel. That resulted in the filing of an assault charge against him (not his first) and his immediate firing.

As he sat across the desk from me, he opened up in a rare moment of honesty. He candidly informed me that he was perfectly happy to stay on welfare. He got to hang out with his friends and receive both money and food stamps. Occasionally, he had to put up with this bullshit, but, hey, he could handle it. He had ways of making a little extra money on the side, which I would never be able to prove, and he regularly got some pussy. All in all, he liked it. He was not about to do anything to find a job or to get himself thrown off welfare, and there was not a damn thing I could do about it. And, you know, he was right.

When it comes to workfare, even if the misguided idealism of welfare policymakers and the perverse attitudes of welfare recipients like Lard Ass do not doom it from the start, labor unions and workman's compensation premiums surely will. The welfare department's strategy involves offering free labor to businesses and industries in exchange for taking on welfare recipients and training them to become productive and employable workers—pass-the-buck strategy. It is also hoped that the employers might even hire the recipients once they are fully trained and prove themselves to be valuable assets—Alice in Wonderland strategy. However, when the labor unions catch wind of this nonunion labor and express their opposition, two-thirds of the potential worksites dry up, leaving only the nonunion worksites.

It then does not take long for these nonunion employers to start questioning the welfare department about who is going to pay the workman's compensation premiums for the workfare workers. And when the department shrugs its shoulders, these worksites also dry up. The employers understand that they will be dealing with welfare recipients who have made it their life's work to know how to bilk the system, and they aren't about to let them substitute their welfare checks for workers' compensation checks. No way!

So, you see, there is actually nothing to surviving workfare because there probably aren't enough work sites to go around. The concept of workfare will always be with us because it sounds reasonable, even though it does not work. Therefore, if you spend any time in the Elephants' Graveyard, you are going to see many incarnations of workfare and may even be required to participate in it. The secret, however, is cooperation. If you just cooperate and wait, workfare eventually implodes and frees you to go back to your previous activities. However, if you lack the patience to wait for it to fail, you can always emulate Lard Ass and appear to be cooperating while actively working to undermine the whole system. I would not advocate hitting anyone in the head with a shovel. Still, a few crude remarks to the local shop steward or some inquiries to the worksite manager regarding the filing of a workers' compensation claim might do the trick.

13 HOW TRAINING PROGRAMS AFFECT YOU

WET BIRD

Wet bird don't fly at night, or wet birds don't fly at night, or a wet bird won't fly at night, or something like that. Given how many times I have heard that phrase, you would think I could recall it accurately. But I can't, and maybe that is because I choose not to.

I'm not sure if my dad invented that droll little saying, but I would guess he did. Somehow, he would always slip it into the conversation. He would blurt out the peculiar phrase and immediately follow it up with, "Think about it." Then his eyes would sparkle as if he had divulged some cosmic secret, and he would sit back and await my response. As a boy, I was always stuck for an answer. As an adult, I'm still at a loss for what to say. To be honest, I doubt I'll ever know what to say. But I still have plenty of opportunities to come up with an acceptable response because he is still making the same odd observation while I remain stuck for an answer.

I mention my father and his peculiar saying because I had an encounter on the way into work this morning that reminded me of him and his twisted perceptions. It happened after I had parked my car and began walking into the city. The rain was coming down in torrents; nevertheless, I trudged on toward the office. Passing along the river, I observed a robin standing contentedly in the rain with a worm squirming in its beak. The robin was totally drenched, and, seeing it, I amused myself with my dad's little saying. I then stood in the pouring rain, staring for the longest time at the wet robin that stood staring right back at me, a true meeting of the minds.

As I contemplated the phrase about the wet bird, I could not help but wonder if it stood there amusing itself with some odd bird saying about wet humans: *Wet humans do not grow rice in the Sahara Desert on Sundays.* But even if it did harbor such thoughts, it did not do so for long. The last I saw of the robin, it was flying off to enjoy its breakfast. I remember thinking to myself how fortunate it was for the robin that night had not yet descended on the city. I was then left with only the rain, the river, and the fog that rolled slowly across the water. The misty fog then caught my attention, and it started me thinking about *The Fog* that was imposing itself on my professional life.

In the last chapter, I talked about workfare, which is actually a component of a broader welfare program known as the Employment and Training Program. The program is more commonly known by its acronym, ETP, but I have always referred to it as *The Fog*. Its stated purpose is to educate and train welfare recipients and then find them gainful employment so they can become independent and productive members of society. Sounds profound, doesn't it? Real profound, especially the first few times you hear it, but then so does the statement about the wet bird. And just as the wet bird, once you start thinking about it or begin looking for results, you begin to see that it doesn't fly. It's all smoke.

Most of the money allotted to *The Fog* is directed toward

education and training. And what are we educating and training these unfortunates to become? Doctors? Lawyers? Indian chiefs? Well, not exactly. From what I can see, we are producing a lot of hairdressers and truck drivers. Beauty academies and truck driving schools are making a killing on this program. *The Fog* continues pumping money and bodies into these educational courses, and the schools keep churning out trained and certified welfare recipients. There is not enough hair in the country or transportable goods to employ all these newly trained professionals, and yet their numbers continue to grow. So the certificates hang on the walls while the welfare checks and food stamps continue to arrive monthly. In the meantime, *The Fog* keeps throwing more money and bodies into beauty and truck driving schools while the welfare rolls steadily increase.

If you are a welfare recipient who wishes to remain in your chosen profession, *The Fog* might seem threatening and intimidating to you. But do not be afraid. It's all an illusion; it has no teeth. Like workfare, as long as you feign cooperation, they cannot do anything to you except make you get out of bed early or stick your hands into other people's hair. They can force you into these training programs, but rarely does the training ever lead to full-time employment and your expulsion from the Elephants' Graveyard. It is like running around trying to put salt on a bird's tail, a wet bird at that. It never gets you anywhere. Now, it's true that some birds, such as owls and other nocturnal predators, do navigate in the dark. But birds, for the most part, do not fly at night, whether they be wet, dry, trained hairdressers, or truck drivers. Think about it.

14 EMANCIPATION

FREE AT LAST!

our score and seven years ago our fathers brought forth ... Wait a minute! That's the Gettysburg Address. I meant to quote the Emancipation Proclamation, but the Gettysburg Address will do for now. They are both associated with Lincoln, and I am sure that Abe's mindset was striking a similar chord when he addressed both of them.

In truth, I do not know much about the Emancipation Proclamation. Oh yeah, I know the standard textbook response that enabled me to pass my seventh-grade civics exam: the Emancipation Proclamation freed the slaves. I am sure that if you had questioned a slave of that period about his newfound freedom, he most assuredly would have replied, "Huh?" But, anyway, during my seventh-grade final exam, I knew the answer then as I know it now. Of course, back then, I did not know anything else about it, and the same holds true today.

The Gettysburg Address required memorization and recitation as an addendum to the final exam, but the

Emancipation Proclamation was neither read nor memorized. Therefore, I can still remember and recite a little of the Gettysburg Address, but I cannot tell you a damn thing about the Emancipation Proclamation except that it was purported to have freed the slaves.

If I remember correctly, I am the one who emancipated Lard Ass. A colleague of mine named Roselyn—or Ros as I called her—always insisted that she had emancipated him, but I knew it had to be me. Hell, I had Annie and Lard Ass' case for ninety-nine percent of the time they were on welfare, so it only makes sense that I would have been the one to emancipate him. Besides, it could not have been Ros. I checked, and at the time of Lard Ass's emancipation, Ros was in the delivery room, making way for her third child. So, that settles it. I emancipated Lard Ass. Of course, I did it without all the fanfare, pomp, and ceremony that probably accompanied Lincoln's proclamation. Like the slaves of Lincoln's era, if you had asked Lard Ass about his emancipation, he undoubtedly would have responded, "Huh?" But then Lard Ass responded that way to almost everything.

I often wonder if Lincoln shared my feelings of hopelessness and futility when dealing with emancipation. Admittedly, Lincoln was acting on a slightly higher plane than I was. He had the issue of slavery to confront and an entire nation dependent on his leadership and judgment. I had only the likes of Annie, who, in her quest for more welfare money, tried to con me into handing down a mandate of emancipation so her minor son could collect a full welfare grant as an adult.

To earn emancipation status, a minor must, for one reason or another, live apart from his parents and be solely responsible for his actions, or, as we welfare professionals spoke of it, he must live *outside the care and control of the parents*. This *care and control* statement was used so often that it was usually abbreviated as *C/C* in the narrative section of a welfare case record.

The intent of the emancipation policy is honorable because sometimes it happens that children are orphaned, put out, or abandoned by their parents before reaching adulthood, and some of these children are capable of directing their own lives from that point forward. This early onset of maturity may be thrust upon them by their circumstances, or their circumstances may be a direct result of their early maturation. But regardless of the conditions causing their independence, when these minors fall on hard times and attempt to collect welfare, the system has a safety valve built into it that allows them to be treated as adults and obtain the necessary benefits. All that is required is for a caseworker to determine the appropriateness of it based on the situation and then bestow emancipation status on the child.

I was always a hardliner when it came to emancipation. It was my belief that you first had to live apart from your parents and gainfully support yourself for an indefinite period of time before you could qualify as an emancipated minor. Moving out and taking a job that lasted only three days did not, in my book, make you eligible to collect welfare as an adult. And moving out of your parents' home without any gainful employment certainly did not qualify you as emancipated.

However, many of my fellow caseworkers did not share that view back then, and the same holds true today. They will grant emancipation to a kid if he can demonstrate the ability to tie his shoes without his parents' help. If a minor moves out and can obtain an address, they will grant him emancipation status and welfare benefits. Often, he moves out without any money and manages to secure housing by promising to pay the first month's rent with his first month's welfare check.

The worst part of emancipation is that once it is granted, it can never be revoked. The minor can then move back in with mom and dad and continue to collect welfare for himself as an adult rather than a dependent child. An emancipated minor receiving welfare as an adult collects more money than he would as a dependent residing in his parents' home. It is that old *care and control* thing again. It is surprising how many parents will admit their failure as parents to obtain more welfare money.

So, it is not hard to understand my annoyance when one of my clients' kids would set up housekeeping in another caseworker's area and deceive the bleeding heart caseworker into granting him emancipation status, after which he would immediately return home to live with my client, and I would have to acknowledge his new status. Or if he did not do that, he would try a common ploy first attempted by Annie and Lard Ass.

Lard Ass erected a tent in Annie's backyard and raised the C/C flag to see if I would salute. I responded by sending him a Salvation Army blanket along with a copy of the Farmer's Almanac predicting a long, cold winter. Two days later, the tent was down, and Annie sent him off to another caseworker's neighborhood to try his luck there. She knew that—similar to my own limited understanding of the Emancipation Proclamation—the other caseworkers did not know or care much about welfare emancipation policy, and they would probably give her what she wanted, namely, Lard Ass' emancipation. Come to think of it, maybe it was Ros who emancipated Lard Ass.

If you are underage, you might think emancipation is the way to go, but you need to be aware that there are dangers associated with it. Once emancipated, you are viewed as a single, responsible adult. And without any deprived children under your care, you could lose your eligibility for federal cash assistance (AFDC and, more recently, TANF). Some states give no money to single individuals, while other states grant their own state-funded welfare. Even in states that do grant State Assistance, not every single adult qualifies. Sometimes, it is paid only to particular age groups (e.g., under eighteen and over forty-five), and limitations are often imposed on how long it can be received (e.g., ninety days every twelve months). As enticing as emancipation might seem, it is always a smart idea to examine the State Assistance rules and requirements before throwing off those shackles and declaring your freedom.

15 PASSING ON YOUR HERITAGE

ROOTS

Here I go talking about Annie again. That is understandable since she was not only an endless source of amusement but also the biggest pain-in-the-ass I ever met. She was, after all, the Mother Superior and matriarch of my caseload during my years as a caseworker. Like it or not, everything revolved around her. The description *Mother Superior* is particularly apropos because she was individually responsible for more resultant welfare cases than any woman I have ever known.

Ros, my aforementioned colleague, once joined me in an attempt to map out Annie's family tree. We began with Annie's name in large, bold letters right at the top. (Annie always liked it on top and would settle for no other position, according to one of her ex-husbands.) The crude diagram then branched off for four generations. It took us a while to record everything because the width of the paper could not accommodate all the names due to the tree's horizontal spread. Eventually, after attaching additional pieces of paper to the sides, we managed to squeeze in everyone's name. By then, four other caseworkers had joined us, and we all began adding identifying demographics under the names of Annie's progeny. Some of the caseworkers then started writing personal comments about many of the individuals included in the family tree.

By the time we had recorded all the names, demographics, and comments, the makeshift collage was gargantuan. Although the top of the tree was only as wide as one letter-sized piece of paper, the bottom section consisted of ten pieces of paper taped or stapled together. It was shaped like a jagged, grotesque pyramid. Color was introduced through the use of multicolored markers, and the whole exercise then turned into a group art project. When the names began to disappear amid a kaleidoscope of information and comments scribbled around them, one caseworker used her artistic talent to highlight and aesthetically improve the lettering. As a result, the names came to develop individual personalities as unique as those they represented. But of all the names, Annie's was the most colorful and ornate.

Upon completion, the giant abstraction was tacked onto a bulletin board while we all reclined to admire our work. It was not until that moment that some rather disquieting revelations became apparent. For one thing, it was shocking that, in a mere four generations, so many individuals could have resulted from the doings of just one woman. Although we knew this to be the case, being faced with it collectively in such a clear illustration was overwhelming. But what we found most disturbing was the fact that all the names staring back at us had been born and raised as recipients of welfare and, in all probability, would remain recipients of welfare for the rest of their lives. Each individual was, in turn, the founder of another family tree composed of multitudes of offspring that would be taught the lifestyle of welfare in order to establish their own trees in the ever-increasing forest of public assistance.

As all this began to sink in, we found it too depressing, and we eventually drifted off to our desks to work on whatever it was that had previously engaged us. Annie's family tree was left hanging on the bulletin board as a reminder of the futility of the system. It remained there for months. Occasionally, someone would make an addition to it when one of Annie's grandchildren had another illegitimate child, and I always made sure to pen in Annie's new last name when she landed another husband. It also served as a stress release when Ros or another caseworker would write in a derogatory comment about one of Annie's children, who happened to be a source of irritation at that moment. But for the most part, it just hung there, claiming a rightful place among the other agency-issued posters and bulletins until it fell down or was removed by the office director for being politically incorrect, unprofessional, and childish.

Where government policymakers and welfare professionals (such as my colleagues and I) might find the hereditary nature of welfare disturbing, that does not mean you have to share our sentiments. It is only natural to want your children to follow in your footsteps while bettering themselves financially, and the system makes it easy for them to do just that. Although I did not follow the same vocational path as my father, he still took pride in the fact that I worked fewer hours and earned more money than he ever did.

It is no different in the Elephants' Graveyard. Parents residing there also like to see the next generation achieve a higher standard of living than the previous generation. And if the past portends the future, it is safe to assume that your children can also claim a spot on the national hammock while collecting more welfare entitlements than you ever did. They say "the apple does not fall far from the tree," so you can sleep well knowing that your little apples will receive all the care and nurturing they need to grow into strong, vibrant trees on which their children and their children's children can sling their hammocks.

16 COPING WITH WELFARE REFORM

DONNA REED

While I was writing this book, some wide-sweeping changes in the guise of welfare reform proposals were being bandied about in the U.S. Senate and House of Representatives as well as in the media. Of course, it was an election year. While the older William Jennings Bryan types stood in the hallowed halls of Congress and lectured their sleeping colleagues on what a disgrace the welfare system had become in the United States, some younger, junior congressmen were busy in a house subcommittee trying to do something about that very thing. What they came up with were some well-intentioned welfare reform proposals for which the senior senators and congressmen immediately claimed credit.

As commendable as these reform proposals were, they were doomed to failure from the start. Except for their political value in promoting or lambasting a candidate in the upcoming election, they had no real positive impact, except perhaps for some peripheral fallout from the election in the form of increased public awareness of the need for welfare reform.

Change is extremely slow or nonexistent in the Elephants' Graveyard, and welfare reform bills necessitate change. As such, they are usually doomed from the start. Welfare exists with a life of its own, continuing at its own pace, unaffected by the minor bickering of congressmen and senators. All claim to hate it, and they promise to do something about it, but rarely is anything accomplished. The minute people genuinely try to address the issue, they are bombarded with complaints and criticisms, and they eventually throw up their hands in disgust. It's okay to complain about welfare, but forget trying to change it. That's why I knew the proposed welfare reform would be as ineffective as all the other previous welfare reforms: it required real change, and that simply was not done.

The senators and congressmen thought they were proposing something new, but it was no different from any of their past reforms. Work registration and training were at the heart of it, as they had been the crux of every proposed reform package dating back to the Democrats' invention of the welfare system. Of course, they always called it something different. This time it was labeled "Ending Welfare As We Know It." However, it was always the same thing: work registration and training with the goal of moving people off the welfare rolls and into productive, self-supporting employment.

This new onslaught of proposed changes had barely hit the press when the critics emerged and pounced. I do not know where they come from, but they always appear on the scene, ready and waiting with prepared rebuttals in hand. This time, the central thrust of the criticism came from a group of liberal zealots who found it necessary to stick their noses into an area where they had no real authoritative knowledge. (But what else is new?) They were upset because it was proposed that single parents receiving welfare—mostly mothers—be required to go to work, or at least seek work after their youngest child attained the age of three. In other words, they were upset with the whole premise of the reform.

I had lived in the Elephants' Graveyard long enough to see how the inhabitants rear their young. Unfortunately, the critics had not spent as much time thrashing around the graveyard as I had, so they had a slightly different perception of the landscape. They objected to the mothers being forced out of the home to seek and find work because they had an idealistic vision of the welfare household, similar to the old 1960s *Donna Reed Show*. It was a place where Donna Reed was home cleaning, cooking, and raising her children, thereby making her modest abode sanitary and happy. Each month, she would pick up her welfare check and food stamps and go to the store to stock her kitchen with the foods that would keep her family nourished and healthy. Through her own good example, she taught her children responsibility and self-reliance, and she prepared them to enter society as productive individuals. Her presence in the home was the cornerstone of her children's upbringing, and she performed her maternal duties with selfless determination and commitment.

Well, not exactly. A more factual illustration might show her at home smoking them cigarettes, yakkin' with them neighbors, watching them soaps, possibly even screwin' them boyfriends while her kids run wild and learn to fend for themselves. Heaven forbid the children be placed in the hands of trained professionals for a few hours a day to learn what Donna was not teaching them. Heaven forbid that Donna should go to work and learn some responsibility, which she could pass on to her children if only by example. Heaven forbid that Donna obtain some education and training, or at least be instructed in the methods of responsible parenting. The critics seemed to ignore the fact that not all "single parents" in the United States receive welfare because many of them realize that survival and growth necessitate that they leave the household to support themselves, their children, and the economy.

Welfare is the essence of the Elephants' Graveyard. It is always going to be a fact of life there, and, hence, so is work registration and training, because work registration and training are intrinsically tied to the receipt of welfare and every reform measure that comes down the pike. I refer only to work registration and training and not to work per se because, if you are untrained, there are no jobs for you out there. Therefore, "welfare reform" typically amounts to nothing more than registering you for work and possibly making you attend some bogus training classes.

Regardless of whether it is work registration or an education/training program intended to lead to work, it never kicks in until your youngest child reaches a certain age. Therefore, the secret to avoiding work registration and training is to start cranking out those children so you will always have at least one child under the threshold age. And since the critics are going to see to it that you are allowed to stay at home, you will have plenty of time to hone your reproductive skills in between reruns of the *Donna Reed Show*.

17 THE NAME GAME

KENTUCKY FRIED CRABS

Several years ago, I made the acquaintance of a couple who live about an hour south of me. We met at the marina where I kept my sailboat and where I spent most of my summer weekends that year. Sunny afternoons would be spent gliding serenely across the water, but in the evenings, back in the marina, we would sit around on the boats and talk about what had transpired during the past week, or we would regale each other with stories from our pasts.

The couple once shared a story about their early years when they had begun dating. At the time, they each had young children—ages four to six—from previous marriages, and they brought them together for the first time on a weekend trip to the Maryland shore. The father, a former Baltimore native, had expressed to the kids his love of steamed crabs and his anticipation of returning to Maryland crab country.

Both of them were relatively young at the time, and neither had much money. Therefore, having spent most of their cash on a hotel room and a trip to an amusement park, they found themselves short of funds, enough to purchase gas for the six-hour journey home but not much more— definitely not enough to buy steamed crabs for which the children had begun clamoring.

Since the children had never before eaten steamed crabs and, likewise, had never been to a Kentucky Fried Chicken restaurant, my friends devised a plan. They made a quick dash through KFC and picked up a bunch of chicken thighs, which they presented to the children as Maryland steamed crabs. The "crabs" were a hit. The kids loved them, and they never forgot the trip.

Years later, when the children were grown and attending a family holiday gathering, they began reminiscing about their first time eating steamed crabs. Overhearing their conversation, the mother blurted out, "Those weren't crabs! Those were chicken thighs! Didn't we ever tell you?"

Outrage is the only way to describe the reaction of the now-adult children, who then began verbally assailing their parents for being deceitful. One of their best memories had now become one of their worst, and no family get-together from that day forward passed without one of the kids bringing up the matter of how their rotten, no-good parents had lied to them.

I mentioned earlier that food stamps are no longer called food stamps. They are now a benefit of the Supplemental Nutrition Assistance Program, or SNAP for short. Because the entitlement descriptors "Food Stamp Program" and "food stamps" had become so tarnished and repugnant to the public due to all the fraud and abuse, the administration decided to change the names rather than enact any real reforms to the entitlement program. They believed that renaming the entitlement program would be enough to make it more palatable to society in general. And so the Food Stamp Program became the Supplemental Nutrition Assistance Program, and food stamps became SNAP benefits. It is far easier to change a few words on official publications and a couple of names on government forms than it is to perform the real work involved in making substantive changes. That is the motto of the Elephants' Graveyard.

Well, this name change may have fooled a bunch of politicians and bureaucrats into thinking they had achieved some comprehensive welfare reform. However, the welfare clients and the other inhabitants of the Elephants' Graveyard know too well that SNAP benefits are still food stamps (only in an electronic form), and they continue to call them food stamps. So, during your sojourn in this strange land, you should be aware that names and definitions are forever changing as the politicians and administrators pull one bait-and-switch after another to mislead the public. Therefore, always bear in mind that whatever is being renamed or rebranded is exactly the same as it was before, and you and everyone else are just being fed a false diet of Kentucky Fried Crabs.

18 PUBLIC ASSISTANCE ELIGIBILITY MANUAL

THE BOOK OF JOB

Welfare is a strange phenomenon. Its premise is benevolent and its aim admirable, but something is amiss in its execution. That is because it has assumed such a monumental task as trying to meet the needs of society's most vulnerable citizens. To be fair and equitable to all involved requires considerable organization and effective management. My advice has always been to gather the welfare clients and their children around the outsides of the county welfare offices each month, and then drop all the welfare money from the rooftops of the buildings. Those with more children (i.e., those with greater need) would have more hands to catch the falling money, allowing them to walk away with a larger share of the month's offerings. Single individuals would only get what they could pull from the air themselves. Of course, the welfare police would be there to maintain order and ensure that no one is hurt. To this day, I continue offering my practical advice, but the welfare administration insists on ignoring me. They instead rely on the Public Assistance Eligibility Manual.

Even more mysterious and bizarre than welfare itself is the method used to determine how benefits are disbursed: the Public Assistance Eligibility Manual. It is called a manual, but it is actually a series of manuals, or rather volumes of manuals. Nowadays, they are volumes of electronic manuals. However, in the past, they were printed publications. They are similar to law books and written about as clearly. There is at least one for every program, with some manuals addressing multiple programs due to the overlap of rules and regulations. Although the regulations often overlap, they are rarely cross-referenced. Of course, caseworkers are expected to know and understand everything contained in each and every manual.

The information and regulations contained in these manuals come mainly from the federal government. Some things are left up to the states, but these are tightly regulated with the governing guidelines coming from the Feds. So, on the whole, the entire manual owes its existence to the federal government. The Feds, however, do not write the manual. Instead, they create laws and regulations that trickle down to the states, which then develop a set of written procedures published in some sort of welfare eligibility manual.

The whole process is quite complicated, but, in a simplified explanation, it works something like this. Laws enacted by the U.S. Congress and welfare changes proposed and published in the Federal Register are all codified into a book called the Code of Federal Regulations. The Code of Federal Regulations is a compilation of new and existing policies, serving as the guiding framework for states to develop their welfare programs. It cannot be used in its existing form because it is unreadable and almost impossible to comprehend, so the states must interpret it and convert it into a more practical tool.

In my state, the Code of Federal Regulations is translated into a more readable format and published in the Public Assistance Eligibility Manual. All new policies and changes to existing regulations must follow this process, which is long and complicated from beginning to end. If you were to trace a policy change from a congressional bill to the Public Assistance Eligibility Manual, you would quickly understand why the whole system fails to work.

Only one thing is sure about the Public Assistance Eligibility Manual—it is bound to change and change quite frequently. Before the advent of electronic editions, caseworkers were constantly ripping out old pages and replacing them with new ones as the regulations changed on a daily and sometimes hourly basis. Ros always filed the latest pages, but that is as far as it went. She knew that they would become obsolete five minutes after she had filed them, so she did not waste her time reading any of them. Therefore, her manuals were always up-to-date, but she had no idea what they contained.

She operated solely on what she had been taught at her initial hiring. Fortunately for her, no one else knew enough to challenge her method of doing things. If you questioned her after noticing her doing something unusual, she would adopt a superior attitude and advise you to reread your manuals. Coya! She would then storm off to her desk, leaving you to wonder if you had not overlooked some new policy change. But, instead of looking it up in the Public Assistance Eligibility Manual, you usually just started doing it Ros' way. Eventually, almost everyone fell prey to her charade, and the entire office became consistent in doing everything the same way—Ros' way (i.e., the wrong way). Well, not everyone.

Clarence had the only practical strategy for keeping track of the changes and knowing what policies and regulations were currently in force. He did not adhere to Ros' methods, and he was the only one who knew enough to tell her that she was full of—well, elephant excrement. His approach was eccentric, but it worked. When I needed a correct answer, I always turned to Clarence.

I should also point out that the department typically provided training to the caseworkers whenever key policy changes were enacted. Unfortunately, the training sessions always proved so dry and dull that no one could stay awake. Consequently, few were able to absorb any of the information presented. To keep from nodding off, many would frantically scribble down every word that was said, hoping it would make sense later on. It never did.

Clarence, on the other hand, was not one to record everything that was said in these training sessions. As a matter of fact, he never even brought paper or a notebook with him. Armed solely with a Styrofoam coffee cup, he would march confidently into the training room. If it were expected to be an extra-long and involved session because of significant changes in the welfare laws, he would bring an extra-large cup of coffee—a sixteen-ouncer.

Clarence had the ability to distinguish between what was essential and what was not, what had to be remembered and what could be ignored. And he ignored a lot. But when he encountered something significant, he made a brief note on his Styrofoam cup. Then, when another piece of policy seemed pertinent, he noted that on the cup as well. Usually, by the end of a training session, the skin of his cup was covered with policy references, clarifications, and reminders about how to implement the changes. It's funny, but I never saw him run out of space. Just when it seemed he would need a larger cup, the session would end. I could never understand how he planned it so well, but then I could never understand Clarence or his mastery of welfare knowledge.

Upon completion of the training, the caseworkers would be released to implement the policy changes that had been addressed in the training session. Unfortunately, most caseworkers did not understand what they had been taught, and they certainly could not decipher their notes. So the pages of notes usually found their way into the trash cans, and everyone went back to doing it Ros' way, except Clarence, of course.

Clarence would return to his desk with his Styrofoam cup and place it amid his collection of other Styrofoam cups. He would then begin implementing the policy changes precisely as instructed during the training session. To my knowledge, he did not even possess a Public Assistance Eligibility Manual, but his desk and shelf space were overrun with annotated coffee cups. If you went to him with a question, he would generally spout off the correct answer without batting an eye. But, if he were uncertain, he would think for a moment and then reach for a cup that would provide the answer. He had some secret bookkeeping system governing the organization of the cups that spanned his fifteen years as a caseworker, and he always knew right where to look to find the answer. Consequently, Clarence always did the right thing as far as his job was concerned, and his clients always received all the benefits to which they were entitled.

The federal and state governments continued to revise the welfare laws, playing havoc with the whole system in what I considered a concerted effort to trip up Clarence. Still, they were never successful, and he never once faltered. Until his retirement, he continued to rely solely on his cups, and his clients continued receiving their welfare benefits in a timely and correct manner. The rest of us, however, almost lost our minds trying to keep up with the changes while we filed new pages in our manuals and made futile attempts to issue at least some welfare benefits to our clients. And since none of us understood the Public Assistance Eligibility Manual or Clarence's coffee cup system, we had no choice but to do it Ros' way.

The Public Assistance Eligibility Manual is a double-edged sword: it can either help or hurt you. The thing you need to understand is that your caseworker probably doesn't know what it says. Therefore, if you can find some way to get your hands on it, or at least some electronic access to it, you can keep yourself abreast of all things to which you are entitled. That way, if you see you are being denied something, you can bring it to the attention of your caseworker by quoting line and verse from the Public Assistance Eligibility Manual. Likewise, if you notice something harmful to your placement on the welfare hammock that your caseworker has overlooked, you can keep quiet, hoping she continues to do things Ros' way and stays away from Clarence. Of course, all this is going to require some industriousness on your part as well as considerable research and a lot of work, things strictly frowned upon in the Elephants' Graveyard.

19 MONTHLY REPORTING

PEN PALS

As a caseworker, I used to see each of my clients at least once every six months, and even that occasional contact I found displeasing. I would have preferred not to meet with them at all and handle everything over the phone, but I was not permitted that luxury. It was required that I meet with them face-to-face every six months, or their welfare benefits would terminate, in which case they would be in to see me anyway due to the nonreceipt of their welfare checks. So, every six months, I sent out notices for them to stop in and see me about keeping their cases active. That way, I at least knew when they would be coming into the office so I could prepare for them. During their six months of eligibility, they were supposed to report any changes in their circumstances, but they never did. That doesn't mean they did not drop by to see me during that time because they did—constantly—and it drove me out of my mind.

Like all other welfare offices, my office was centrally located in the area it served. That made it convenient for the clients, but I viewed it as a nuisance. For some reason, my clients felt the need to stop in and say hello whenever they were passing by, which was all the time since the office sat amid their homes. Often, they would accompany their neighbors and seek out my companionship to pass the time while their friends were meeting with other caseworkers. That may seem sweet and special, but social work is not the order of the day in welfare offices anymore. It is strictly income maintenance work where the primary goal is to ensure that cash assistance, food stamps, and Medicaid find their way into the hands of the clients. There honestly is no time for anything else. But still, when a client pops in, he must be seen, even if it is his eighth visit that day.

There were many reasons why my clients stopped by to visit. Most of the time, they wanted to ask if they qualified for more benefits. Often, it was to show off what they had bought at the store. And one client even stopped in to ask if I wanted to tag along while he looked for a new apartment. I respectfully declined. Rarely, however, did anyone come in to report a change in circumstances, such as a marriage, a change of address, the receipt of an inheritance, or a job. I was always amazed at the number of radical changes that took place in the lives of my clients at the exact moment I would send out the six-month appointment letters for updating their eligibility. People got married. People got divorced. Babies popped out of the womb. Children went off to live with their grandparents. Clients found jobs. Clients mysteriously lost jobs. And I never questioned any of it. None. Nada. That's because I was glad they had waited to report it at their six-month interview and had stayed away from me the rest of the time. Then, just when I had them all trained to avoid the office and not bother me, the department initiated *Monthly Reporting*.

Monthly Reporting was mandated by the federal government, and it was designed to make the clients report changes in their circumstances. Although it affected everyone receiving and disbursing welfare benefits, it was actually targeted at the unscrupulous clients, who declined to report anything, and the lazy caseworkers, like me, who did not want to be bothered even if things had been reported. The Monthly Reporting System forced the clients to at least report. Report what? Something, anything, it didn't matter. It didn't even have to be truthful. It just had to be reported.

Reporting forms were mailed to the welfare clients from the state capital each month. To avoid having their cases terminated and benefits shut off, the clients had to complete and return these forms to the local welfare offices by the deadline date. This influx of reporting forms into the welfare offices immediately became a workload issue for the caseworkers, who had to process them by another deadline date or the cases would automatically close, causing the clients to come charging into the office, looking to rip out the lungs of the beleaguered caseworkers. Needless to say, neither the clients nor the caseworkers liked the system.

The Monthly Reporting System had a few other drawbacks. First, it assumed that the clients could read, and that was not a safe assumption to make in the Elephants' Graveyard. It also assumed that the clients could follow directions, another assumption that could never be made in the Elephants' Graveyard. And finally, it assumed that the caseworkers would be conscientious about implementing the rules governing Monthly Reporting, and that would get you laughed right out of the Elephants' Graveyard. To make matters worse, the Monthly Reporting forms had to be one hundred percent complete and submitted on time, or the welfare benefits stopped dead in their tracks. As a result, I had my illiterate clients running into the office each month to ask, "What does this say?" and my confused clients stopping in to ask, "What does this mean?" and the rest of them dropping by to ask, "Do you like the new shoes I just bought?"

The stated goals of the Monthly Reporting System were as follows: 1) to free up more of the caseworkers' time; 2) to generate a current source of client information; and 3) to provide the clients with a tool for reporting changes in income and circumstances. This reporting system, they figured, would provide an efficient method for sharing information without the constant running in and out of the office that ate up the caseworkers' valuable time. Reporting forms were generated and mailed to the clients every month, and the forms had to be completed, signed, and mailed back to their caseworkers in the envelopes provided. Pretty easy, right? Wrong.

The final result was the exact opposite of what had been envisioned regarding the Monthly Reporting System. The clients did not like the system, did not understand the system, and did not cooperate with the system. The caseworkers also did not like the system, understood it about as well as the clients did, and were about as cooperative as the clients were. This led to even more office visits to address the problems caused by the Monthly Reporting System, as well as the clients' failure to take it seriously. The caseworkers then spent ninety percent of their time dealing with client visits and Monthly Reporting concerns, and their other job functions and responsibilities were left to hang fire. Gone were the days of only seeing a client once every six months; the clients were continually visiting the office courtesy of the system that had been designed to keep them out.

Nothing that begins in the Elephants' Graveyard ever truly ends. It took the department about twenty years to recognize the problems caused by the Monthly Reporting System and to revert to the six-month client-contact policy. But they could not let go of the written reporting requirement entirely. They decided to retain the reporting form itself—the one no one could read or understand—and they called the new system *Semi-Annual Reporting,* or SAR for short. Because of the continued use of the reporting form, SAR failed to alleviate—and in some cases exacerbated—many of the problems experienced under the Monthly Reporting System. Where Monthly Reporting used to send out all the reporting forms the same day each month, SAR began staggering the mailings throughout the entire month and throughout the whole year, precipitating a constant, never-ending parade of clients coming into the office every month. And to think, I used to get upset when they would just stop by intermittently to say hello or show off their new shoes.

The welfare department is obsessed with reports and reporting. Reports are its essence, as they are for any bureaucracy, and they are something you cannot escape. Whether you are a resident or an employee of the Elephants' Graveyard, you are going to feel the sting of the reporting mandates. It is just something you will have to accept, and all you can do is grin and bear it. Regardless of how you feel about your caseworker, the department is going to insist that the two of you become pen pals. On a regular basis, you will have to disclose to your caseworker what is going on in your life, and most likely you will have to do it in writing. That, however, does not mean you cannot stop by the office to shoot the breeze or show off your newly purchased shoes. I'm sure your caseworker will be happy to see you. It's not as if she has anything better to do with her time.

20 ELECTRONIC BENEFIT TRANSFER

WHAT'S IN YOUR WALLET?

I already discussed some aspects of the Food Stamp Program, and I previously mentioned how food assistance ceased to be known as food stamps. What I mean is that they ceased to be paper food coupons; the notion of food stamps is never going away. In place of paper coupons, we now have electronic benefit transfers, more commonly known by the acronym EBT. If you are not familiar with this acronym, start paying attention as you drive through town. The signs are everywhere: *We Accept EBT*. They are plastered all around grocery stores, and they're now turning up in corner stores like 7-Eleven and pharmacies like Rite Aid. It seems that everyone accepts EBT these days, and that is by design. When you are attempting to craft a government-dependent society, you need lots and lots of outlets where people can access their government entitlements.

EBT involves the transfer of welfare benefits from the government to the recipient via an electronic transfer, deposited into a pre-established welfare account. The entitlement benefit is then accessed through what is called a "point of service" (POS) electronic exchange at a grocery store or any retail establishment that has been given permission to accept EBT transactions and has obtained the necessary technology and equipment to submit the transactions electronically. Bank automated teller machines (ATMs) are also used to access the EBT system. The EBT card looks identical to a gift card, credit card, or debit card, and that is also by design.

EBT does not refer specifically to food stamps. The other welfare entitlements are also accessed using the EBT card. In fact, the EBT card has become the preferred method for distributing almost all welfare entitlements, including cash assistance and Medicaid. Food stamp access via EBT, however, is more recognizable because the public can easily observe food stamp exchanges.

Each week at my local grocery store, I observe over and over again the person in front of me paying for her groceries with an EBT card. Then, I turn around and look at the person waiting behind me, and, sure enough, she also has her beloved EBT card gripped tightly in her hand. Since I'm familiar with the card's appearance, I can easily spot one, but the average person probably cannot. Those unacquainted with the Elephants' Graveyard probably think their neighbors are simply charging their purchases on credit cards. But then I wonder if there remains anyone in society who has not yet become acquainted with the entitlement subculture. Perhaps I am the only one still buying my groceries with real cash.

Once, when I was a young adult and had been working day jobs for six months, I fell into financial need when the work abruptly stopped. At that time, I took a cash assistance check for a month, but then quickly landed a full-time job. The people at the welfare office did their best to try to convince me to take the food stamps as well, but I refused. My refusal was not based on any strong moral objection. In truth, I was too embarrassed by the whole situation, and I did not want my friends and neighbors to see me forking over paper food coupons at the grocery store. At the time, I also never told anyone about the welfare check. Come to think of it, this might be my first admission ever! Regardless, if things had been then as they are now, I could have accepted and used the food stamps without anyone being the wiser—no stigma, no embarrassment, no pain. And like I mentioned before, that is all part of the grand design.

If you are experiencing the same hesitation I had back then about venturing into the Elephants' Graveyard, you need to push those doubts aside and proceed boldly into that strange land. Take solace in the fact that the overseers of the graveyard are working to remove any and all obstacles and stigmas associated with your chosen entitlement, and the EBT card plays a significant role in this effort, as it represents a major step toward normalizing all things welfare-related.

There is the old saying that goes something like this, "If it looks like a duck, walks like a duck, and quacks like a duck, it must be a duck." Well, I say if it looks like a gift card, purchases groceries like a credit card, and dispenses funds from an ATM like a debit card, it could be an EBT card—or a credit card—or a debit card—or a gift card. Only you know for sure.

21 ADVANCE NOTIFICATION

TROUBLE ON THE HORIZON

I have never put much stock in fortune tellers. Magicians amaze me, and I will even admit to believing that some of them actually do disappear when they vanish from the stage, but fortune tellers do not elicit the same degree of awe where I am concerned. I know many people who regularly consult with fortune tellers, but I most assuredly do not. Once, however, I was attending a Halloween party where a fortune teller was present as part of the entertainment, and, like everyone else, I received a personal palm reading. She told me that I would soon have a falling out with the girl attending the party with me. As it turned out, she was right. But thinking back now, it did not take a fortune teller to spot that one. The only other prediction I remember her making has yet to make itself known one way or another, and I am not in any real hurry to find out.

After she had finished trashing my love life, she asked if I had any questions. I didn't, but to keep the conversation going, I asked the first thing that popped into my head,

"Will I have a long life?" I said it half-jokingly, certainly not expecting a reply. To my surprise, I got one. Tact was not one of her strong points, and she told me point-blank, "No." Of course, at that moment, I jettisoned my disbelief in fortune tellers and drew back my hand, peering into my palm.

"What do you mean, 'No'?" I asked while continuing to stare at my hand. What did she see in there that I did not? She then proceeded to explain how she disliked delivering unwelcome news, but to protect her credibility, she couldn't lie. And not only did she tell me that I would not live to a ripe old age, but she also added that I had been lucky to remain on the vine for as long as I had. It was then that I realized why I did not like fortune tellers: I do not want to know what is going to happen to me.

I do not believe I am unusual or alone in my aversion to knowing future events. If they are truly delightful and wonderful happenings, well, then, that's a different story. But when was the last time something delightful and wonderful happened to you? And how often do those types of things occur? More often than not, whatever is destined to befall you tomorrow will probably be pretty mundane, and there is a strong likelihood it will be unpleasant. The next significant thing to turn your life upside-down is most likely not a lottery windfall. That's why I don't want to know what is going to happen to me. If I know beforehand, I'll just worry about it until it happens. Without knowledge of the future, all I can do is wait for the next thing to happen and deal with it when it does. Maybe, in the meantime, I can squeeze a little enjoyment out of life. As I mentioned before, I don't think I am alone in these sentiments.

Other people may share my viewpoint, but bureaucracies are not people. The Department of Public Welfare has this notion that everyone is visiting fortune tellers and wants to know the future. For that reason, it insists on notifying welfare clients of all future negative happenings well in advance of when they will occur. I have always believed that this is not so much to allow them the opportunity to prepare for the worst, but rather, to rob them of whatever peace of mind they might have left. For example, young, single men who in the past used to qualify for ninety days of welfare payments were handed their termination letters at the same time they were approved for benefits and issued their first checks.

But issues that adversely affect cash assistance, food stamps, and Medicaid are not the only things about which the clients are notified. They are sent advance written notification regarding anything and everything related to their cases—good, bad, or inconsequential. It matters little that they have no comprehension of the things about which they are being informed or that it makes no difference to them one way or another. Regardless, the caseworkers are required to inundate them with notices and letters informing them of everything that may or may not affect their receipt of welfare. For example: *This is to notify you that our state has terminated a welfare reciprocal residency agreement with the Republic of Bulgaria.* Perhaps it is a blessing that the clients cannot read.

I have often thought how terrible it would be to receive advance notification of all the unpleasant consequences awaiting us in our lives.

This is to notify you that the following trials and tribulations will be inflicted upon you over the course of the next eighty years:

1. *You will be accident-prone throughout your life and eventually break every major bone in your body.*
2. *You will become an alcoholic and fail at everything you attempt.*
3. *Your only son will be gay.*

4.   *Your wife will insist that you are too dull and leave you for an accountant.*
5.   *You will be falsely imprisoned for a crime you did not commit and spend the remainder of your days on a chain gang.*

A former colleague of mine once devised a method to save the state a significant amount of welfare money by utilizing the advance notification letters. According to him, all we had to do was send letters to all the welfare recipients in the state. The letters would read, "Your welfare benefits are being terminated, and you know why!" He concluded that the honest clients, those who did not know why, would immediately contact us to ask why, and we would simply apologize and instruct them to disregard the letters. Some of the dishonest clients, the amateurs scamming the system, would realize they had been caught and would remain silent as their benefits terminated—and we would know why. The true professional scammers, however, would call and feign outrage. These ones would get to stay on the welfare hammock because we were never going to catch them anyway. But at least we would get a few of the bad guys off the rolls.

My colleague proposed this action in jest, but I took it seriously. I thought it was brilliant, and I initiated the next step by writing it up as a formal proposal and sending it to the secretary of welfare. I immediately received a curt reply informing me that my current civil service status was in serious jeopardy, and I knew why!

My coworker also had a few other off-the-wall ideas for welfare reform, such as requiring welfare recipients to don orange jumpsuits and earn their welfare checks by acting as stand-ins for the orange hazard barrels along the road at state highway construction projects. But after the stiff rebuke I received from the secretary of welfare over my advance notification proposal, I decided not to forward to her any more of my colleague's ideas.

As distasteful as it may seem, you will have to allocate time in your busy schedule to sort through the enormous deluge of mail sent to you from the welfare office and left on your doorstep each day. Most of the correspondence you will not understand, and much of it will not apply to you. But now and then, they will send a letter that portends impending doom if you do not take some required action to stay on the national hammock. That is where many people slip and fall off. They either cannot or do not read the mail coming from the welfare office. Also, you never know when the secretary of welfare might relent and decide to implement my proposal by having the government fortune tellers blanket the Elephants' Graveyard with fake termination letters just to see what happens. And if you receive one, you will now know why.

22 WELFARE RIGHTS

RENT-A-MOB

At one point in my youth, during my early teens, block parties became the rage in my hometown. Of course, my neighbors insisted that our street participate. Committees were formed, and people were assigned varying duties and responsibilities to make it come together in one well-orchestrated event. The street was closed and barricaded by city employees, tents were erected, tables and chairs were carefully arranged, and an overabundance of food was prepared. Games were planned for all the children, with a few adult games thrown in for good measure.

My father worked for the city in the engineering department at the time, and he borrowed a megaphone from the police for use in supervising the children's games. He brought it home after work on the day before the block party, and it provided my friend and me with several hours of entertainment that night. I had never held or used a megaphone before, and it amazed me how powerfully it amplified my voice even when I spoke in a subdued tone.

Later that night, when my friend left to return home, I watched him from my bedroom window as he walked through the backyard to his house on the next block directly behind mine. I waited until he was just about to his back door when I stuck my head out the window and spoke into the megaphone in as deep a voice as I could muster, "Gary, this is God!" He practically jumped out of his skin because, as he later admitted, the sound was so booming and pronounced that he thought I was standing just inches behind him.

The most seductive thing about a megaphone is the feeling of power it imparts to the user. When you pick it up, you are immediately aware that you can out-shout anyone at any time. In fact, you feel as if your voice could reach the outer limits of the galaxy, and that is almost true. When I said to my friend that night, "Gary, this is God," I think I actually believed I was God.

I never again had the opportunity to use a megaphone after my block party experience. That may have been a good thing, as it seemed to evoke mega-maniacal tendencies in me. However, I have seen and heard them used by others over the years. My closest encounter with one came while I was working in the Elephants' Graveyard as a caseworker. It occurred on a rather typical day while I sat at my desk idly pondering what people with real jobs do at that time of the day. And then it started. All I could do was sit and stare in stunned disbelief.

It was back when I was a relatively new employee, and security wasn't a significant concern in the offices. The door from the reception room into the interviewing area was always left unlocked, and that is how they gained access. "They" were a parade of people, the lead members of which were all alien to me. Those at the end I recognized. They were the clients from the reception area who had decided to join in when they saw the procession forming. The lead members carried tambourines and maracas, and they danced, chanted, and clapped their way through the interviewing area and into the heart of the office, where the employee desks and cubicles were laid out in one huge room.

At the head of this bizarre conga line was one incredibly fat woman with a megaphone. What she was saying was indiscernible because the earsplitting decibels of the unintelligible sounds bounced off all four walls and collected in a medley of screeches, echoes, and reverberations in the center of the room. It was apparent that the user of the megaphone was feeling the same sense of power I had experienced in my teen years at the block party. I remember thinking, *Who are these people?*

As it turns out, "these people" were the local Welfare Rights Organization that had organized a public display to make their presence known. Well, they made their presence known all right. At least I never forgot them. I'm also sure they achieved their objective, that being intimidation. You knew right away that these people were crazy, and you wanted no part of them. You would do whatever you had to do not to deal with them, and that is precisely what they wanted. I am not saying I would not enforce some portion of welfare policy out of fear of retribution from the Welfare Rights wackos, but I'm sure there were caseworkers out there who thought twice about doing anything that could cause a backlash. It's possible these caseworkers might alter their actions to avoid such problems.

The people in the Welfare Rights Organization might be crazy, but crazy can be a good thing if you choose to inhabit the land of the Elephants' Graveyard. You need to have crazy on your side because, sometimes, that is the only thing that can save you. Modern-day welfare is a crazy phenomenon, so crazy can prove a worthy ally. You should view the Welfare Rights Organization as your version of a union. It uses the same tactics and attracts the same types of people as unions. Hell, they may even be the same people.

Regardless, they will do whatever it takes to keep your entitlements coming, whether you are eligible for them or not. If nothing else, you will get to clap your hands and shake a tambourine, and, if you are lucky, you may even get to experience some real power by singing and chanting into the megaphone.

23 ONE MAN, ONE VOTE

VOTER FRAUD INC.

I walked into the Bureau of Motor Vehicles to renew my driver's license. The renewal required a new photograph, so I needed to appear in person. While a female employee at the counter shuffled through my renewal papers, she glanced up briefly and asked if I would like to register to vote. I told her that I was already registered, so she returned to shuffling her papers. I stood at the counter for a few moments, thinking to myself before asking her this question, "What would have happened if I had agreed to register to vote?"

She glanced at me over the top of her glasses and raised her head slightly. Her face then assumed a grimace that can only be achieved by a government employee when asked to do something connected with her job. She inhaled and exhaled deeply before explaining that I would need to complete everything on an accompanying form, which she then handed to me. Otherwise, I only needed to check the box and sign where it said: "I do not wish to register to vote."

I took a few moments to peruse the form before commenting, "But there is nothing here about proving my citizenship. How do you know I'm eligible to vote if you don't require me to prove that I'm a citizen?" I was already aware of the National Voter Registration Act of 1993 (commonly referred to as the Motor-Voter Bill), and I knew I would be offered the opportunity to register to vote. I was just curious about the answer I'd receive if I asked what every real American should ask when confronted with this situation.

Once again, she expelled a sigh before explaining that it was not her job to determine citizenship. She was only told to have the form completed. If people in the Voter Registration Office at the courthouse wished to verify the qualifications of any would-be voter, they were free to do so. But in the end, it was not her job or her concern, period.

Well, I thought, you cannot get any more matter-of-fact than that. Welcome to modern-day America! But, like I said, I knew all this beforehand. Hell, I had been living it. After all, I worked in the Elephants' Graveyard, where all this was commonplace.

They may have generically called it the Motor-Voter Bill in the U.S. Congress, but the bureaus of motor vehicles were not the real targets of this bill. The actual targets were the welfare offices. That is where the real diabolical nature of the bill came to life. The goal was not to obtain lists of drivers who are registered to vote; instead, it was to get lists of welfare recipients who are registered to vote. Drivers actually go out and vote. Welfare recipients—well, that's a different story altogether. The Democrat members of Congress who passed the bill knew that welfare recipients, for the most part, don't vote. They also knew that by getting them to register, they could secure lists of registered voters who would not be showing up at the polling places on Election Day—in other words, Voter Fraud Incorporated. To verify compliance with the federal Motor-Voter Bill, states must maintain databases of those who agree to register to vote and those who do not. And rest assured, all the wrong people in the political sphere have access to those lists.

If you decide to venture into the Elephants' Graveyard, you need to know that you will be hounded endlessly about registering to vote at every interaction with the department: application, reapplication, change reports, phone calls — any and all contact whatsoever. No conversation or meeting with anyone in the Department of Public Welfare will ever end without someone asking you about voter registration and making you sign a form if you choose not to register. You may find that registering to vote is far easier and more preferable than continually having to respond to inquiries about your voter registration status.

But you need to understand the unstated truth about voter registration in the Elephants' Graveyard. Although you are expected to register, you are never expected to vote because someone is going to do that for you. If you were to vote, you would risk exposing the fraud, thereby collapsing the whole house of cards. Remember, the people giving you the freebies are the same ones using your vote to stay in power. It is the classic quid pro quo. They get to keep their cushy jobs, and you get to remain on the hammock. They receive all the expensive perks while you scrape by on a few lousy welfare checks and some food stamps.

24 LEARNING THE LANGUAGE

WINDTALKERS

Here in the grand old USA, we love to use acronyms. How about that? I just used one—USA. Our love affair with acronyms is a direct result of our tendency to blow things out of proportion and make everything seem more significant than it is. A long, confusing name always sounds impressive, so we describe everything with the longest, most difficult names we can find. If a name is also impossible to pronounce, that is even better. But we are a nation on the move, and we do not have time to spell out or pronounce these extraordinarily long names. It is a dilemma. So we start referring to them by their initials, or we assign them shortened names based on words closely associated with their abbreviations—that is, we tend to use acronyms. Soon, things become more defined by their acronyms than their proper names, if anyone can even remember the names by then.

No one abuses this practice more than the government, and no one in the government is more abusive than the Department of Public Welfare. (Or should I say the DPW?)

In the DPW, no one speaks English: they speak *Welfarese*. More correctly, they speak an abbreviated version of *Welfarese* dusted liberally with acronyms. Acronyms grow like weeds in the language of caseworkers and welfare bureaucrats. They use them in both their conversations with each other and with the public. Caseworkers constantly bark out rules and regulations in unintelligible mumbo-jumbo at poor, confused clients, and bureaucrats broadcast the same meaningless gobbledygook over the public airwaves. And the sad part is that neither the caseworkers nor the bureaucrats realize that no one understands a word they are saying, and everyone considers them OTL (out-to-lunch).

I understand the problem, and I know how hard it is to turn it off. Life in the Elephants' Graveyard is a constant effort to be as vague as possible, and it isn't easy to reverse course when you must address a press conference or explain to a client what she must do to receive her Medicaid card. Just writing this book has been extremely difficult for me because I'm a master of *Welfarese* in all its inherent vagueness. I am particularly skilled at the use of acronyms, and I can wield them like a scalpel to pare down the essence of any client's case history into one or two paragraphs. I can also expertly decipher the written language of the Elephants' Graveyard, be it scrawled on a cave wall or neatly recorded in a welfare case folder. The case of Willie Burmer is a perfect example.

The Department of Public Welfare first became aware of Willie when his mother gave birth to him at St. Elizabeth's Hospital. The hospital had her sign a medical assistance application prior to the delivery, and they sent it to the welfare office with the expectation that Medicaid would pay for her delivery and hospital stay. When the signed application arrived from the hospital, Willie's mother was scheduled for an appointment at the welfare office to complete the application process.

At the appointment, federal cash assistance and food

stamps were authorized, as well as Medicaid for both her and her newborn son. The required advance notification letters were sent to both the hospital and Willie's mom. Since Willie's father did not live with his mother, she was referred to the Domestic Relations Office so she could pursue child support. Due to Willie's infancy, his mother was not required to seek employment. Willie was also not required to register for employment until he reached the age of eighteen.

The years passed, and life progressed normally for Willie as a child on welfare. He entered public school, but he only attended for eleven years. When he dropped out, he was registered for work and placed by the Job Training Partnership Agency into an on-the-job training program at the state university in the maintenance department. This eventually led to full-time employment and the termination of his public assistance case. He was sent an advance notification letter explaining why his case had closed.

But things soured for Willie. He developed a minor drug problem, but he still managed to keep his job. Then, after four years, he was laid off, and his minor drug problem became a serious one. He collected unemployment compensation benefits, leaving him with too much time on his hands. This furthered his addiction problem and, for the most part, caused him to be unemployable. When his unemployment compensation benefits ran out, he applied for workers' compensation and Social Security Disability, but he was denied both. It was then that he sauntered back into the welfare office.

He was not the same Willie upon his return. Whatever self-esteem he had possessed as a child was now gone. He was bad-tempered and irritable. Yet, despite his sour disposition, he completed a welfare application and was determined eligible for cash assistance. Because he was now over the age of twenty-one, he no longer qualified for federal cash assistance, so he was granted state-funded cash assistance in a category called *transitionally needy*. That category meant he could only receive ninety days of cash assistance per year unless he could produce some medical documentation of a disability. He was sent notice of all this on an advance notification letter.

Before his ninety-day termination, Willie informed the welfare office of his drug problem, and he supplied a written doctor's statement to back it up. His drug addiction qualified as a disability, and the category of his cash assistance was changed to *chronically needy,* meaning that he could continue receiving cash assistance beyond the ninety days and for as long as he needed it. He was also referred to a drug and alcohol clinic for rehabilitation. The continued receipt of his cash assistance was dependent upon his cooperation with the counselors at the clinic.

But poor Willie never had an opportunity to be rehabilitated. Shortly after being referred to the clinic, he was diagnosed with AIDS, acquired through his unsanitary habit of syringe sharing. That certainly qualified him as being disabled, and his state-funded cash assistance case was closed because he then qualified for federal Supplemental Security Income administered by the Social Security Administration. The state still handled his Medicaid coverage, so the welfare office continued to maintain a case record on him. He was sent the appropriate advance notification letter advising him of all this.

Not long after that, Willie died. His Supplemental Security Income benefits were terminated, as was his Medicaid. In both instances, the required advance notification letters were sent, but like all the other notification letters that had been sent to him in the past, these too remained unread.

If you pull Willie's case record out of the dead file (no pun intended), you can read an account of everything I just reported. It might not look the same or even make any sense to you, but it is all there. To the untrained eye, it will look like gibberish, but to someone schooled in the language of the Elephants' Graveyard, it will appear normal and quite understandable. Willie's whole life story, as previously related, can be summed up in this:

> CAF and MA 913 rec'd St. E. Appt Notice sent. AFDC, MA & FS author. 162 to LN 01 & St. E. DRO refer. LN 01 CS & ETP-2. LN02 ETP-1 till 18. LN 02 PS 1-11/DO & Man ETP. JTPA/OJT PSU. AFDC, MA & FS closed. 162A. L/O PSU. UC exhaust/WC & RSDI denied. Into DPW & S.O.B. Auth TN-GA/90 days (inelig AFDC-over 21). 162 PA 816 rec'd MD-drug addict. TN-GA closed/CN-GA auth. D&A refer. Diag. AIDS. Closed GA/open SSI. 162C. Closed SSI/MA. 162C. D.O.A.

During World War II, the Japanese army had become quite adept at breaking the communication codes developed by the United States armed forces, that is, until the military leaders recruited Navajo Indians from the American southwest and trained them to use their native language as code for communicating on the battlefield throughout the Pacific Theatre of Operations. The Japanese were never successful in breaking that code, and we all know how things turned out for them. Metro-Goldwyn-Mayer (MGM) Studios made a movie about those Navajo soldiers in 2002, which was entitled *Windtalkers*.

The language of welfare, with its overuse of acronyms, might not be as complex as the Navajo language. Still, to the untrained eye, it can seem nothing more than a jumble of letters and sounds arranged in strange and confusing combinations. But you, as a welfare Windtalker, battling in the theatre of the Elephants' Graveyard, must be able to decipher the code in order to read your case record and discern what your caseworker is saying about you and what dangers lie ahead.

25 ENERGY ASSISTANCE

THREE DOG NIGHT

I used this expression once already because I like it, so I've decided to use it again with a slightly different twist. If it looks like a duck, sounds like a duck, and smells delicious roasting in my kitchen, it must be a duck. Right? Well, maybe not. Despite my fascination with that duck aphorism, I understand that it can't be appropriately applied to all situations, especially those encountered in the Elephants' Graveyard, where reason and common sense are in short supply.

Energy Assistance is a social program designed to provide financial assistance to people in need—looks like a duck. The federal government funds it and ultimately controls it—sounds like a duck. And it is enacted through the state governments by their departments of public welfare—hmm, just smell that bird roasting in the oven. So, why is it not considered welfare? Well, actually, it is, but it is only considered welfare by those administering the program, not those receiving it. Recipients of energy assistance think it is—well, I am not sure what they believe it is, but it certainly is not welfare.

I am calling it energy assistance because that was the common name for it when it started in the late 1970s and early 1980s. I think they also called it home heating assistance. Nowadays, it bears the name Low Income Home Energy Assistance Program or LIHEAP for short. Because it is aid for paying heating (and now cooling) costs, it does not carry the stigma of cash assistance, food stamps, and Medicaid. For some reason, people believe it is entirely appropriate—and almost expected—that the government subsidize their utility bills. But when the government steps in and subsidizes shelter, food, and medical expenses, well, that is something entirely different.

It is a commonly held belief among recipients of energy assistance that welfare involves only the receipt of cash assistance, food stamps, and Medicaid; energy assistance is a whole other animal. To them, it is not even welfare with a small W, and they will become belligerent at the slightest suggestion that welfare money is paying their gas bills. They castigate the "lazy welfare bums," but they are the first in line each autumn when the energy assistance applications become available. During my time as a caseworker, I let them play their little rationalization games while I did my best to process their energy assistance applications.

To qualify for energy assistance, two conditions must be met and verified. First, it must be confirmed that the family has an annual income within the allowable limits. Second, the family must demonstrate that they incur an "identifiable heating expense." Eventually, that also came to include an "identifiable cooling expense." The Feds have always had a relaxed definition of what constitutes heating and cooling expenses, and the reason is so that more people can be determined eligible to participate in the program.

I was also as flexible as the Feds in allowing people to participate in the program when I processed energy assistance applications. I once even considered granting energy assistance to a man based on his dogs. He could not produce a heating bill or any documentation verifying that he incurred a legitimate heating expense. (This was before you could qualify with a cooling expense.) He did, however, insist that his home had a heating source: it was the heat supplied by the three Great Danes that slept with him at night. He then presented me with a breakdown of all the expenses required to keep them heat-producing. He even brought the three of them into the office to verify their existence. It was a compelling argument, one I had to respect. Anyone who could come up with an angle like that, I decided, deserved the money. Besides, from the look and smell of him, it was clear that he was actually sleeping with those dogs.

The state must have liked my liberal interpretation of the energy assistance rules, as policymakers decided to outdo me. Welfare, you see, is very incestuous by its nature, and many of the welfare programs play off one another. One program will automatically recognize you as eligible based solely on the fact that you qualify for another program. By applying for just one entitlement, you can unlock a series of additional entitlements in other programs. Additionally, receiving an entitlement in one program often qualifies you for more of another entitlement in a different program. Although the energy assistance recipients do not believe their benefit to be welfare, the policymakers know exactly what it is, and they are experts at playing the qualification game.

Based on the way food stamps are calculated, everyone receiving energy assistance automatically receives a greater food stamp benefit amount. The state policymakers, however, decided to take it a step further. They first identified every food stamp recipient in the state who was not receiving energy assistance. Then, with a wave of their magic wand, they granted many of those people one dollar's worth of energy assistance funds that then qualified them for more food stamps. Voila! It could not have been easier. They were not concerned that many of those people did not qualify for the dollar, did not want the dollar, and were unaware that they had received the dollar. With the EBT system, it was hard to tell where the money was coming from anyway. The state proudly dubbed the scheme the "Heat and Eat Initiative." I dubbed it "insanity."

So let all of this be a lesson to you if you find yourself tiptoeing through the Elephants' Graveyard, worried about offending the wrong people and fearful that your meal ticket might be revoked. The reality of the situation is that most people running the system are essentially on your side, and sometimes, unbeknownst to you, they will go far out of their way to get you more (e.g., the Heat and Eat Initiative). As for energy assistance, unlike some of the recipients who are in denial, you need to understand what it truly is—your entitlement—and you must be prepared to take advantage of it. And unless you have assumed room temperature and are being carted out in a hearse, you can always make the compelling argument that something is keeping you warm at night, and you need money to pay for it, even if it is just a Sterno stove, the hooker down the street, or several large canines.

26 EMPLOYMENT AND TRAINING REDUX

THE FETAL EMPLOYMENT PROGRAM

I already discussed the Employment and Training Program and its specific components, such as workfare, when I talked about my dad's Wet Bird idiom and introduced you to Lard Ass. I'll now address it again because it's a key initiative in public welfare, something the welfare reformers always propose. Unfortunately, it's a goal they never achieve. Still, they try over and over again to implement it with the same unfortunate results. Therefore, as a citizen of the Elephants' Graveyard, you will be exposed to it repeatedly in its many incarnations, so it's essential to understand its true nature and origin to prepare yourself for the worst.

Many refer to the Employment and Training Program by its acronym, ETP, but I always called it *The Fog*, as I mentioned before. Unfortunately, my pet name describes it far more accurately than any word in its official title. *The Fog* originated in Washington, D.C. Need I say more?

It was the brainchild of some enlightened legislators who

thought they had come up with a novel approach for addressing the problems of welfare. "Let's get them jobs!" someone said on the Senate floor one day. "Jobs? What a great idea!" another senator chimed in. "These people would prefer to work rather than collect welfare." (It was apparent that they had never met Annie or Lard Ass.) "Let's pass a law to that effect," added a third senator. So they passed one of the many welfare reform acts that ordered the states to get these people off welfare and into jobs. It was then the seventh day, so the lawmakers went home to rest: welfare reform is hard work.

Acting out of desperation and under the threat of money sanctions imposed by the new welfare reform law, my state, like many others, used all the guidance and support offered by the federal government (which amounted to nothing) to establish the Bureau of Employment and Training (which was next to nothing), or rather, *The Fog*. *The Fog* then rolled out over the state, obscuring everything in its path.

Its intended purpose was to find jobs for the employable welfare clients and provide job training to the unemployable clients. The training aimed to turn unemployable clients into employable clients and eventually employed former clients. A noble proposition, but unrealistic. This objective and its unlikely outcome had always been the implicit goal of welfare, whether officially stated or not, and it also had been one of the great fallacies of welfare. A great truth of welfare is that those who find jobs and get off the welfare rolls do so of their own volition. But, unfortunately, that reality was not known to the lawmakers, or else not believed by them. So, with all these profound truths and fallacies already known, the actual objectives of the Bureau of Employment and Training came to be as follows: 1) hiding the truth and 2) perpetuating the fallacy—fog tactics.

Whether from a client or employee perspective, contact with *The Fog* was always the same. It would roll by, but you could never clearly distinguish anything. *The Fog* was simply too dense. You would hear sounds and voices, but the words communicated nothing: it was just noise. There appeared to be a lot of activity, but little was getting done. At that time, I had already left the county welfare office for another job, so I called back to see if Annie and Lard Ass were still around or if they had been placed into jobs—they were still there, and they had no jobs. And *The Fog* crept slowly along.

It did not take the state long to realize the futility of trying to achieve the stated goals of *The Fog*. They were also quick to recognize that the Feds were more interested in statistics than success. One statistic that intrigued them was the number of welfare clients who had been registered for work. That was something tangible. That was something they understood. That was something they could easily verify, with "easily" being the keyword. Therefore, work registration became the principal determinant as to whether or not a state was in compliance with the welfare reform law, and the Feds enforced that provision by mercilessly doling out federal sanctions when they discovered a client who had not been registered.

They mandated that the states maintain a registration index of employable welfare clients who were supposedly seeking employment. If a state failed to keep a registry or include all the employable clients, it faced substantial fines and risked losing federal funding for its welfare programs. After being slapped down several times by the Feds, my state was desperate to come up with a way to ensure that all the employable clients would at least be registered for work. Several plans were proposed, but each had built into it the potential to miss large groups of employable individuals whom the federal auditors would undoubtedly discover.

The problem lay in who the Feds considered employable. As with anything government-related, the policy was not straightforward regarding who met the employability requirements. Various exemptions existed that took into account age, sex, education, marital status, family size, and other factors. As a result, many mandatory registrants slipped through the cracks due to welfare office oversights, misinterpretations of the policy, or simply due to the laziness of caseworkers. All the brilliant minds in the state bureaucracy were beside themselves about what to do until someone came up with an idea.

The simplicity of the idea contributed significantly to its elusiveness. It was almost too easy, and, for that reason, no one believed it would work. The federal mandate required that states register all employable welfare clients for work, but nothing more than that—no training, no job search, no work. It became clear that the Feds were not looking at anything beyond the act of registering people as available for work. And a closer examination of the mandate also revealed that the Feds had no prohibition against registering unemployable welfare clients. It only said that employable clients must be registered for work; it made no mention of those who were unemployable. Therefore, the simple solution to the problem was to register everyone.

And that is what we did—we registered every welfare client for work. A new definition of "work registration" was established, and new procedures and forms were created to implement the registration process. Work registration became necessary and automatic for everyone currently receiving welfare benefits and all those applying for benefits. Both adults and children were registered, and the policy wording was changed to indicate that once registered, you were registered for life. The simple act of signing the application for welfare benefits was all that was needed to complete the work registration of everyone in the family. Nothing more was required. Then, being forever paranoid, the state took it a step further. It began registering the fetuses of expectant mothers to avoid accidentally missing them when they popped out of the womb, and these too were registered using their mothers' signatures on the welfare applications.

Nothing was ever done with the registrants, and there was never any danger of their getting jobs because work registration only involved collecting their names and putting them into a data file for the rest of their lives. The funny thing was that the Feds accepted this. They accepted the state's definition of work registration and its process for registering clients via their signatures on the welfare applications. To them, it appeared legitimate because the state was maintaining a database of all the registrants. It mattered little that no use was ever made of the information or the lists. It also did not seem to bother them that the names on the lists remained there for all eternity. The work registration requirements were being met, and that was all that mattered.

As a result of this sham, the threat of a federal sanction in this one area of compliance was removed forever. Gone was any future danger of being fined for something that involved work registration, and that made a lot of people in my state's Department of Public Welfare quite happy, as it did the Feds in the Department of Health and Human Services. With everyone automatically registered for work, how could the federal auditors discover anyone who was not? They could stop looking, the state could stop worrying, and Annie and Lard Ass could return to their lives of comfort without anyone needlessly hassling them about something as distasteful as work.

There is a complaint about welfare, alleging that it dehumanizes people and creates dependency in them, much like a narcotic drug. It's true that the children of welfare recipients grow up to become welfare recipients, and I found it sad and amusing that my state had discovered yet another method to indoctrinate them at an even earlier age. I certainly do not expect it, but if there is ever a shortage of fetuses in the job market, I know right where to look.

So, you shouldn't let it disrupt your nap if your

caseworker tells you that you are being registered for work, because nothing will surely come of it. Just light up a cigarette and recline leisurely on the hammock as the balmy breezes of the Elephants' Graveyard gently rock you back to sleep. And if anyone tries to disturb your restful bliss with some crass or defamatory statement about how welfare recipients should be out looking for work, proudly tell them that you are currently registered for employment and doing everything required to get a job. And not only are you registered for work, but so are your children, and even your expectant child. Come to think of it, so are your next three children yet to be conceived! And if they still give you any guff, simply flick your cigarette butt at them, and offer them this subtle but always appropriate rebuke, "Coya!"

27 CASEWORKERS

FRIEND OR FOE?

I began my tenure in the Elephants' Graveyard working in a temporary position with *The Fog*. I had been an out-of-work school teacher, and I took the job to tide me over until I could find another teaching position. Well, I never landed that teaching job, but I managed to leverage the temporary job into a permanent full-time caseworker position. I then spent the next thirty-two years held captive in the Elephants' Graveyard. My first assignment as a caseworker was in the Intake Department.

"Intake" was the name given to a group of caseworkers that did not maintain caseloads but, instead, processed all the new applications received from people applying for welfare benefits. Afterward, the new clients and their case records were forwarded to "continuing eligibility" caseworkers for case maintenance. However, before that, the Intake caseworkers first had to schedule appointments with the applicants, meet and interview them, and complete all the necessary forms and paperwork to determine their eligibility for benefits. Intake was a special unit, its distinct status recognized by its physical separation from the rest of the welfare office.

Initial eligibility authorizations can be tricky because they determine where the funding will come from; therefore, Intake should be comprised of the best and brightest caseworkers—in effect, the office elite. However, that was not the case in my office. When I was assigned to Intake shortly after being hired, everyone seemed surprised because most viewed an Intake assignment as a form of punishment, a move that brought you one step closer to the door.

Intake had earned the reputation of being the place they sent you when you could no longer function anywhere else because of illness, incompetence, or attitude. In other words, it was the last stop before you disappeared altogether. The person I replaced was one of those who had vanished. He no longer worked in the office, and no one knew (or was willing to say) what happened to him. Whenever I asked about him, the subject was quickly changed, or someone remembered a pending application that needed to be completed before quitting time. All I knew about my predecessor was that he had bequeathed to me a half-filled bucket of water that was left sitting beside the desk.

Intake was situated in a remote part of the building. To travel to the central office that housed the other caseworkers, you had to go up to the second floor, through the clerical office, and then drop down one level to the main welfare office. We were extremely isolated, and very few of our co-workers ever visited us. They knew what Intake portended, and they wished to stay as far away from it as possible. Whenever I found it necessary to journey over to the main office, I always rang a bell before me while crying out, "Unclean!"

Each of us in Intake had a desk and file cabinet, both crammed into a small cubicle that served as our office space and interviewing booth. The entire Intake area was nothing more than two rectangular rooms connected with a doorway and a small window with a sliding glass panel. One room was the waiting area for applicants; the other room was the office area of the caseworkers. Cubicles lined each side of the caseworkers' office space with six-foot metal partitions separating each one, supposedly allowing for privacy. These partitions, however, only eliminated visual exchanges; sound seemed to be amplified by them, and you could easily discern conversations three cubicles away.

A narrow walkway ran down the center of the room between the two rows of cubicles, and it was passable by only one person at a time. It was never possible to traverse the entire length of the room without meeting someone coming the other way, so you were constantly ducking into someone's cubicle, interrupting their interview to allow an oncoming parade of caseworkers, clerks, and clients to pass by. My cubicle was the first one on the left, easily identified by a picture I had hung over my desk: a sepia-toned photograph of some sunbaked elephant bones lying on an arid African plain.

Hilda had the booth next to mine. She was an unusually tall, large-boned German woman who refused to speak of her past. Many suspected that she might be a Nazi war fugitive, but no one dared find out. She was towering and intimidating, and she bore a striking resemblance to George Washington on a dollar bill. Mostly, it was her nose and profile, so I should probably say that she resembled Washington on a quarter. But like our suspicions about her war criminal history, everyone thought it best to keep our George Washington observations to ourselves. It was Hilda who finally showed me why my predecessor had left behind the bucket of water.

Hilda smoked incessantly. As absurd as it may seem to people today, smoking on the job back then was commonplace, and Hilda availed herself of that freedom nonstop. I cannot even picture her in my mind without a cigarette in her hand. And when it was not in her hand, it was dangling from her mouth. She always kept it in her mouth when she wrote, and she insisted on talking without removing it. That, along with her thick German accent, made it difficult to understand her, so I continually had to listen to those she interviewed say "What?" and "Huh?" after every question. Eventually, they would make up an answer when she would repeat the question as imperceptibly as before. What scared me was that I soon began to understand her speech. I then felt obliged to fix her applications after the fact, realizing that the applicants had unwittingly provided incorrect information because they could not understand her questions.

Although Hilda smoked, she had no respect for fire. For her, the cigarettes were a pacifier; they were not an immediate threat to her fellow workers. I do not smoke and have never smoked, but I chew on my pens and pencils. And when I am finished gnawing on them, I throw them away. Hilda also threw away her cigarette butts, and she cast them aside with as much concern as I did my discarded pens and pencils. Consequently, her wastepaper basket would catch fire (hence the bucket of water bequeathed to me by my predecessor). She also had the habit of falling asleep at her desk. As always, she had a lighted cigarette in hand, so the ashes would inevitably fall into her wastebasket. When I finally escaped from Intake, I bequeathed to my own successor a ready bucket of water.

Despite Hilda's pyromaniacal tendencies, she impressed me. She had a way with the clients. Long ago, she had perfected an interviewing technique where she would "gently" coerce them into saying what she wanted to hear. She would lead them down the yellow brick road before unceremoniously cutting them off at the knees. I recall a specific interview that took place after a policy change that eliminated roomers and boarders from the list of individuals eligible for food stamps. The conversation I overheard was pure Hilda.

Hilda: "Are you a roomer and boarder?"

Applicant: "Huh?"

Hilda: "Are you a roomer and boarder?"

Applicant: "Well, ah, no. I give her some money, but, ah, we kind of eat separately."

Hilda: "Are you a roomer and boarder?"

Applicant: "Well, you know, she kinda buys her food, and I kinda buy mine."

Hilda: "Are you a roomer and boarder?"

Applicant: "Well, you know, if I'm home and she's cooked something, well then, sometimes I eat with her, you know."

Hilda: "Are you a roomer and boarder?"

Applicant: "Yes, dammit! I'm a fuckin' roomer and boarder!"

Hilda: "Roomers and boarders are NOT eligible for food stamps! Application denied!"

Jimmy was another one who was banished with me to Intake. It was immediately apparent why he had been sent there, because he was the biggest agitator in the office. I have never been a fan of mimes, but I made an exception in Jimmy's case because he had a real flair for it—a true talent. He knew I appreciated it too, so he always endeavored to keep me entertained. What can I say? I was his biggest fan and always an available audience.

Jimmy was an impressionist, but he was not the kind of impressionist you see on television or in nightclub acts. He did not mimic the voices of famous personalities; he imitated the body movements of the people in our office. His favorite target was Hilda. He had perfected her strut to the extent that you almost believed it was her. He would not say a word. Instead, he would parade in front of whomever he was impersonating, mirroring their walk along with all their idiosyncrasies. They would be totally unaware of the apparent ridicule taking place, which added to the hilarity of the situation. He was an artist, and, for the longest time, I appreciated the stress release his antics provided. Then, one day, I viewed myself on a video taken at a friend's wedding. Immediately, I noticed that my gait and movements matched those of Jimmy whenever he was around me. Suddenly, he wasn't so funny anymore.

The entertainment provided visually by Jimmy was matched vocally by Jerry. Jerry was a music fan, and he could identify the song title and artist of almost every popular song dating back to the 1950s. He could not only name them, but he could sing them as well, something he did continually. This was all right until he took it one step further and began talking almost exclusively in song titles and lyrics. Since I did not have to work closely with him, I could live with his novel vocabulary. Actually, I was fascinated by his ability to do it; however, most others in the office did not share my passion. Later in his career, when he began telling applicants to *Blame It On The Bosa Nova* for the delay in their food stamp benefits, they cut short his musical contract, and he found himself looking for a new gig.

Fascinating, however, is the only way to describe Henry. Some people thought Henry was crazy, but I didn't believe it. Unfortunately, at least for Henry, the office management staff didn't believe it either. My feeling was that Henry wanted out but could not afford to quit. He was also too young to retire. The only other option available to him was to feign insanity, pretending he had been driven crazy by job-related stress. As such, he could then collect workers' compensation or work-related disability. This charade he attacked with enthusiasm and creativity.

His off-the-wall antics were an endless source of amazement and delight. However, his paranoia gag was one of my favorites and quite possibly his best. One day, he announced rather loudly to the entire office, beginning in Intake, that two paperclips were missing from his desk. This was not the first time something had been pillaged from his desk. He had been the victim of thievery for quite some time. It was only now that he decided to speak up. Those two paperclips were his favorites; he had raised them from mere staples. Now, they were gone, and—well—he didn't know what to do. What he did know was that he would be taking steps to ensure that he lost nothing more to theft.

The first step he took involved bringing in an ice pick to scratch his name onto everything he owned. He then acquired some twine and secured everything on his desk and inside it. Next, he tied all the drawers shut. When he ran out of twine, he walked over to the window beside my desk and began stroking the window sash. "You using this?" he asked, looking down at me with a peculiar twinkle in his eye, one that was always there when he was in the middle of one of his performances. I always expected but never received a wink. It didn't matter, though; the glimmer in his eye told all. Both he and I had a tacit understanding of what was going on. Sometimes I think we were the only ones who knew what we were doing.

And then there was Lester. Lester and I were not particularly close, so it is a mystery why he chose me as his confessor. However, he did. I think it was at our office Christmas party that he confided something to me that I wished he had kept to himself. It seemed that he had a problem, which would become especially troublesome during the holiday season. You see, he was a "price-adjuster."

He told me that it had started innocently enough a few years prior, but it eventually blossomed into an uncontrolled obsession. Whenever he went to a department store to shop, he would first determine what he expected an item to cost; however, the proprietors of the stores were never on the same wavelength, and they always priced their merchandise higher than Lester was willing to pay. In those cases, he did some price-adjusting of his own by putting the item on sale. His method for doing so was by peeling off the price label of a lower-priced item and affixing it to the thing he wished to purchase. He claimed to have been doing it for years and had never once been caught.

He then began worrying when he found himself unable to stop. It mattered little whether or not he intended to buy anything; he would wander the stores on his lunch hour and randomly change price labels. While other people perused the merchandise, he canvassed the store in search of loose price stickers. He viewed the whole thing as a challenge. Any shame he experienced was rationalized away by his claim that everything was overpriced. He was, in essence, performing a public service. No consumer advocacy groups for him; he took matters into his own hands and bypassed all the red tape. When he saw something he viewed as obviously overpriced, he adjusted the price to what he felt was fair.

Automation came to his rescue, or Lester would have been bearing his soul to his cellmate instead of me. With the advent of electronic scanning equipment, Lester was forced to end his crusade—at least that is what he said. Where he could easily con a checkout clerk, a computer was not so gullible. During his lunch hour, I would still see him aimlessly wandering the stores, appearing forlorn and miserable. I would never linger long to observe him because I did not want him to see me. Whenever he did, he would run over and insist on helping me with my shopping. He would ask what I was there to buy and rush off to find it for me. I never explicitly voiced my distrust of him in these situations, and I always accepted whatever he had located for me; however, if the store did not use electronic scanning equipment or the item did not have a bar code, I would slyly scrape off the price sticker so the clerk would have to call for a price check. That made me terribly unpopular with the people in the checkout line behind me, but it made me feel better and undoubtedly saved my ass more than once.

Well, it turned out that my Intake assignment was not a secret plot to get rid of me, and I remained there about a year before taking action to get myself moved out of the Intake Department. I was assigned a caseload and relocated to the central part of the office, where I then had to put up with the likes of Annie and Lard Ass. About four years after that, I applied for and received a promotion to a welfare examiner position in another bureau within the Department of Public Welfare, a job that required my leaving the county welfare office and moving to a new office in a larger city. It was like the governor handing down a pardon only minutes before the execution because, just like that, I was delivered from the jaws of a living death and took my leave as quickly as possible.

Before I left to accept my new position, I stopped back in the Intake Department one last time to bid farewell to the old crew. All of them were still there, exactly as I had left them a few years earlier. As I turned to go, I glanced back to witness a sight I would long remember and cherish: amid the glow of Hilda's newly-purchased, burning trashcan (one Lester had bought "on sale"), Jimmy could be seen mimicking Henry as he sat guarding his desk, stroking his ice pick and eyeing the window sash while Jerry belted out a melancholy rendition of *See You In September*.

Many people end up working in welfare out of necessity: it is not something they set out in life to do. Usually, it is something that happens because nothing else presents itself, or people are too lazy to pursue anything else, or they are just too eccentric to work anywhere else. Some people adjust quite well to a working career in the Elephants' Graveyard, and they just lie back and take whatever is thrown at them. The job is essentially a means to an end, providing something to do for the next thirty to forty years until retirement, when they can do at home what they've been doing on the job—namely, nothing. No big deal. But then there are those caseworkers who resent the fact that they are there, and they become bitter and angry at everyone and everything. And lastly, there are some who become caseworkers because that is what they genuinely want to be. These are the idealistic ones who wish to change the world.

As a resident of the Elephants' Graveyard, you must learn to identify the type of caseworker with whom you are dealing and also to determine the caseworker's primary reason for being on the job. Mostly, you will encounter those like my colleagues from the Intake Department, harmless individuals who are a little eccentric, people you can befriend and easily manipulate. They might be easy-going people just putting in their time, or they could be stressed-out zombies pushed to the brink. In both circumstances, their overriding concern is finding the fastest and easiest way to get the job done. So, as long as you can facilitate that quick and easy way, you will be okay. The ones you need to worry about, however, are the angry, bitter ones and the do-gooders.

In any jungle, there are natural predators. The Elephants' Graveyard is no exception. It has its share of dangerous inhabitants that command respect if not outright fear. These predators fall into two categories: 1) caseworkers banished to the Elephants' Graveyard who are not happy about being there, and 2) overzealous, do-gooder caseworkers who are there of their own choice and volition, the ones with the bachelor's and master's degrees in social work. One type is ready to devour you if you annoy them, and the other actually knows the laws and regulations and feels obligated to enforce them on you, which is the same as being devoured. Both types are your worst enemies, and if you find yourself assigned to either one, your outright survival requires that you get your case moved to a caseworker who will serenade you with regulatory song lyrics, teach you the art of pantomime, or show you how to obtain a fifty-percent discount on your next purchase at Walmart.

28 WELFARE POLICE

HAVE GUN WILL TRAVEL

After working five years as a caseworker, I secured a promotion that enabled me to escape the county welfare office, which I mentioned in the previous chapter. Of course, I made my departure as dramatic as possible. With my comrades gathered around me, I packed my saddlebags and rode off into the sunset amid a rush of tears and sorrowful goodbyes. I knew them to be proud of me for the mission I was about to undertake: to rid the state of welfare fraud. It was a mission I wholeheartedly supported and truly believed in. I approached it with a naïve dedication, and I vowed to do all that was asked of me and go wherever the job required. And for all this self-sacrifice, I demanded only what was mine: my meager wages and my pride. Somehow, I felt like Paladin.

As a youth, I had watched a fair amount of television, and the program *Have Gun Will Travel* had been my favorite. I can still see the leather holster bearing a silver chess knight in the opening moments of the show, the image frozen on the television screen before the blackened, headless torso of Richard Boone drew his shiny revolver and pointed it directly at the television audience while issuing a stern warning to that week's villain or any other villains that might be tuning in to that night's episode. Paladin didn't take guff off anyone, and neither would I!

You see, Paladin was a soldier of fortune, or rather, a gunslinger or hired gun. But, most of all, he was a businessman. When he was not dressed in black garb, pivoting around with his revolver to issue stern warnings to villains, he was dressed elegantly, spending his time lounging around the casino of the Hotel Carlton with beautiful women on his arm, the ladies also dressed elegantly. That setting is where he would be found in the opening segment of each week's episode. It is also where someone would inevitably seek him out to solicit his services—for a handsome fee, of course.

Just before interrupting him in the middle of some fascinating tale he would be relating to at least three gorgeous women, the prospective client would always glance down at a business card in his hand, one that explained how he had come to learn of Paladin, prompting him to seek out his services. The card was imprinted with a horse's head representing a chess knight, and the card read: *Have Gun Will Travel ... Wire Paladin ... San Francisco.* In my youth, I was not familiar with telegraphs and had no understanding of wiring someone, so I just assumed that "Wire" was Paladin's first name—Wire Paladin.

As a boy, I had all the Paladin accoutrements: a black hat, a holster emblazoned with a plastic knight emblem, a toy gun, and, most importantly, business cards that looked just like the ones in the television show. I would spend hours standing sideways in front of a full-length mirror, drawing my pistol and spinning around to mimic the show's opening sequence until I could do it as well, if not better, than Richard Boone. My Paladin business cards, I carried with me always. I was Wire Paladin.

So I left the county welfare office and set out like a soldier of fortune in an untamed land, ready to do battle with any and all types of welfare villains. I no longer had my gun and holster, but I had been issued business cards, something that helped fill the void. *Have Gun Will Travel* read the card of Paladin. Unfortunately, my business cards did not read that way, but they might as well have—I still was Wire Paladin.

The mission assigned to our bureau was called Project Integrity by the governor, but I do not think he made that known publicly. We seemed to be the only ones who knew of it, but that was okay. The public might not have known the governor's pet name for us, but it would not be long before everyone knew who we were and what we were doing. Fifty of us were hired and let loose across the state to "clean up" things. The bureau and its mission had been around for a while, but there had never been any field operatives to carry out the task. But now we were on the scene, and things would be different.

The first ones to learn of our presence were the ones who were cheating and bilking the welfare system (welfare villains), and our arrival on the scene made them a little edgy. We targeted the clients collecting welfare benefits illegally: those working jobs without reporting their income; those with unreported resources in the form of property, motor vehicles, and various types of financial accounts; those collecting unreported forms of unearned income; and those claiming desertion by a parent or spouse when the family continued to reside together. These were the ones we went after, and they quickly realized we were around.

The first reaction of the villains was to discredit and ignore us. However, when they saw what was happening to their comrades, they began rethinking everything. Because they had been cheating the system and getting away with it for so long, they felt secure in their belief that our methods would not work. Hell, nothing in state government works! But this was different. It operated off a different set of principles alien to most other welfare initiatives. It was designed for success rather than failure, and succeed it did. Streamlined and specialized, it went for the throat, and suddenly a lot of villains were bleeding all over the place.

After realizing that ignoring us would not work, the next reaction on the part of the villains was simply to disappear. That was okay with us, too, because our primary goal was just to get them out of the welfare system. Often, they would resurface in another county, but we had people there also. They soon came to realize that we were everywhere.

Those who chose not to disappear decided to stand and fight. The length of time they had spent cheating the system usually determined the vigor with which they fought and the kind of battle waged. Some were extraordinarily adept at it, and we could not gather enough evidence to do anything about them. They had learned too well how to hide their tracks. For the most part, however, their scams were transparently childish and unsophisticated. Unfortunately, at least for them, they lacked the intellect to recognize it. Instead, they foolishly considered their fraudulent schemes to be enormously complex and worthy of some defense. What they failed to realize was that their scams had been successful only because no one previously had the time to rout them. Well, we had the time, manpower, and resources, and rout we did.

When hiding or fighting did not work, the villains tried the only thing left in their arsenal—they cried and whined. It is a well-known fact in the Elephants' Graveyard that if you cry, whine, and complain loud enough, and if your cries and complaints reach high enough into the bureaucracy, you get whatever you want. This is especially true if you can escalate your complaints to the level of the secretary of welfare or governor, in which case, you might even land a bureau director's job.

So complain the villains did. They complained about our tactics. They complained about how we spoke to them. They complained about how we looked at them. They complained about my labeling them as villains and issuing them stern warnings. They even complained about the weather. Luckily, it was a Republican administration, and their complaints fell on deaf ears. After all, we were Project Integrity, and we were making the system safe for the good citizens of Welfareland. Paladin was a hired gun, and, as such, his methods were not always above reproach. However, he got the job done, and so did we.

We targeted a particular county and typically worked it as a team of two. Sometimes, however, we worked independently. I preferred to work alone because that's how Paladin worked. When in a county, we stayed four months before moving on. Then, in about a year or a year and a half, we would return. Just when the villains thought it was safe to collect welfare again, we were back. The caseworkers liked us. The Republican administration liked us. Hell, even many of the inhabitants of the Elephants' Graveyard liked us. Only the welfare villains did not like us, and that was the whole idea.

Our division chief shared my equally romantic view of our mission, rooted in my Paladin fantasy. He envisioned us kicking open doors, hauling out the bad guys, and handing them over to the local authorities. We would then rear up on our horses, creating silhouettes against the setting sun (a scene reminiscent of my departure from the county welfare office) as we rode off in search of new welfare adventures. He often referred to us as "the guys in the white hats." Before the death of Roy Rogers, when he was in town attending the grand opening of one of his restaurants, I ended up with an autographed picture of him waving his white hat while rearing up on Trigger before a flaming sunset. "Happy Trails, Roy Rogers and Trigger," it read. We immediately adopted Roy as our mascot, and I hung the picture on my desk. Secretly, I would have preferred to have had Paladin as our mascot, but I accepted Roy, keeping Paladin as my own personal role model. After all, I was Wire Paladin.

The most remarkable thing about Project Integrity was that it worked and got results—at least for a little while. A few years after our inception, there was a change of administration from Republican to Democrat, and the new governor appointed a new secretary of welfare, who in turn appointed a new bureau director and division chief. It seemed that the outgoing governor forgot to tell his successor about Project Integrity because we started hearing all this talk coming from the state capitol about "too many policemen in the state," and suddenly, people began to jeer at our hard-earned results and cost savings. No one could deny that we were helpful and that we were saving the state a bundle, far in excess of the cost of our salaries and benefits. In fact, we did such a fantastic job that the federal government agreed to pay one-half of our wages due to all the money we saved the Food Stamp Program. In a word, our organization worked, and it worked well.

I guess things are never supposed to succeed in a bureaucracy or in the Elephants' Graveyard. They are designed for failure, so that's what they do. And when they do fail, no one is upset because the failure was expected all along. It is only when something succeeds that it becomes a threat, as it shines a light on all the other failures and prompts everyone to ask why. Questions are tolerated even less than success, so we cannot have anyone asking why.

That's what happened to Project Integrity. It did what it was supposed to do, and it did it well, so action was taken to make it fail. The whining and complaining of the villains reached officials in the new Democrat administration, who did everything in their power to console the whiners. That consolation entailed revoking our "license to kill" and substituting softer duties for us to perform in the bureaucracy. They never actually eliminated our bureau or Project Integrity; instead, they gave us other tasks to focus on. Once something starts in the Elephants' Graveyard, it continues forever. Project Integrity still existed, but no one was assigned to it. Like Paladin, we were back in the casino wearing our fancy clothes and spinning tales of past welfare adventures while awaiting someone to solicit our services.

As you roam the Elephants' Graveyard, be alert for the hired guns that occasionally appear and traverse the nether regions of your world with the ability to create havoc in your life. Take comfort, however, in the knowledge that there is no real passion for them to succeed, so they will eventually fade away. As I mentioned before, things in the Elephants' Graveyard seem to have a life of their own and never actually die. As administrations change, you will see the welfare police resurrected now and then, but their presence on the landscape and their impact on your lifestyle are usually fleeting.

29 SPECIAL AUDITS

BETTY'S LEGS

I think it was Rodney who first brought them to my attention—Betty's legs, that is. It was not like he had a fetish with women's legs in general; his obsession seemed to focus solely on Betty. At the mere mention of her legs, he would go weak-kneed and begin to melt right before your eyes. Most of it was put on, but there was a deep-seated lust that always found its way to the surface. It was this hint of true passion that glistened in his eyes when he was talking about her celebrated legs. Not only his eyes, but his whole body seemed to delight in mentally caressing the objects of his desire. He would shrug his shoulders and sleepily close his eyes. Then, he would pucker up and squint before drifting off into a dreamlike state. At that point, he would groan gutturally, "Oh, those legs!" Unfortunately, I never got the chance to appreciate them the way Rodney did because, every time I looked at Betty, the only thing I saw was red.

For a short season in my career, I was afforded the opportunity to make a positive impact on the Department of

Public Welfare instead of sitting around complaining about how badly it was run. I was sent to the state capital to work for a year "on loan" in our headquarters office. This temporary assignment involved the development and implementation of a special audit that had been requested (or, rather, mandated) by the federal government. My job was to design a methodology by which we could determine how well our state was implementing one aspect of the Food Stamp Program. Admittedly, I was not going to change the whole system with this assignment, but I was damn sure it would be done right. Additionally, I would not let it become a bureaucratic circus like many others I had seen. I intended to achieve results, and I was ready to put forth the extra effort that would be required. My authority was coming directly from the federal government, so no one should challenge me. I was a man on a mission, singularly driven, and I knew I would succeed. What I did not count on were Betty's legs.

The stated purpose of the audit was well-intentioned, as are most things originating in the Elephants' Graveyard, even if the final results do not end up that way. I was to develop a method for determining whether clients were being reissued food stamp benefits after being "cheated" out of them for one reason or another. Since most clients lack sufficient knowledge of welfare policy to understand their entitlement to food stamps, the department is responsible for policing itself to ensure that everyone receives the correct amount. My job was to police the department to ensure that it had, in fact, been policing itself. I found the assignment challenging and exciting, and I was eager to begin.

I lived about a five-hour drive from the state capital, so the time I worked there—commuting every week—was somewhat of a strain. However, I knew the sacrifice to be worth it, and the hardships associated with the excessive driving made me even more determined to develop something meaningful. And I did it. I worked hard and developed methodologies and procedures to do precisely what the Feds expected us to do—evaluate our system for restoring food stamp benefits to eligible households. It was a lot of work, and I was given a free hand in it because it was a lot of work, and not many government employees will jump at something like that. In a bureaucracy, if you are willing to do the work, most everyone is willing to let you do it.

In the end, however, I found it baffling because it seemed too easy. I then wondered why more successful programs weren't being developed, given how easy it was. Admittedly, during this period of my career, I was somewhat proud and thought quite highly of myself. Still, I knew I could not be the only competent employee in the entire Capitol complex. There had to be other capable people around. As much fun as I made of the department, I knew it could not be entirely devoid of talented, conscientious, and success-oriented people. So why wasn't quality work being produced? I then caught sight of them out of the corner of my eye—Betty's legs.

I was told, probably by Rodney, that she shaved them twice a day. On more than one occasion, I observed her coming from the ladies' room, jamming something into her purse that appeared to be a razor. I would look over at Rodney, and his eyes would be fixed on the doorway, waiting for her to walk by. He knew her schedule, and I swear he had it programmed into his body clock. He did not set any alarms or have to be told, but he knew the precise moment when she would appear. He would then be waiting, all puckered up and oozing with lust as she walked by. "Oh, those legs!" he would softly whisper.

Anyway, I developed the audit and then assumed the unpleasant job of explaining it to others. Since the entire state had to be canvassed, I could not do it alone. For that reason, several colleagues of mine from our field offices were assigned the task of implementing the assessment. I would explain the process and objectives to them, instruct them in the methodology and procedures, coordinate their assignments, and then use the collected results to report to the Feds at the conclusion of the audit. Since we had been allowed one year to complete the process, and since I had used only four months developing the audit, we had the remaining eight months to carry out the field activities, obtain the results, figure out what the results meant, write the report, and submit it—a piece of cake.

I used to be a school teacher, and I also worked for a time as a training specialist in the Department of Public Welfare. I do not know if I mentioned that before, but I will point it out now. I only reference it here to indicate that I am no stranger to imparting information to large groups of people. Because of that, I was not anxious or nervous about training my colleagues. I had spent four months developing the audit, so I knew it inside and out. I then spent another week organizing the material and writing a training syllabus. I was fully prepared. I even retired to bed early the night before the training session so I would be alert and energetic the next day. But even though I had everything going for me, something unexpected happened that upended things in the training session. At the time, I did not know what it was, but I do now: it was those legs.

She walked into the room and plopped her rump into a chair before crossing those gams. Had I been more seasoned in the politics of headquarters, I would have known what to expect. But I was the new kid in town and much too amused at Rodney's reaction to Betty's entrance to realize that I was in real trouble. I do not know if Rodney realized it either. If he did, it was hard to detect through all his oozing and squinting. Those legs. Those delectable legs. They would prove to be my downfall. And there they were, pointed directly at me.

Maybe I should tell you a little more about Betty, things

that do not concern her notorious legs. She was in charge of one of our larger regional offices, but she maintained workspaces in both the headquarters office and her regional office. I had never had any previous dealings with her before accepting the temporary headquarters' assignment. Since she worked so far away from me, I had never before seen her or her legs. To me, she had just been a name in our bureau directory, but now I had some legs to attach to that name. There was no real reason for her to be at my training session that day, but she had decided to attend just to stay involved, keeping her finger on the pulse of things that might impact her regional office.

A finger I would not have minded, but she had to stick those legs in, and the session turned into chaos. It is not easy to take nothing and make something out of it, but it is surprisingly easy to ruin everything someone else has created by pointing out all its flaws. And that was Betty's forte. With a minimum of knowledge, she began pointing out everything she disliked about the audit and everything she wanted changed. I had spent four months researching, analyzing, testing, and weighing alternatives to determine the best course of action, so it is understandable how upset I became when Betty whimsically rejected the bulk of everything I had presented and demanded that it be done in a manner that she spouted off the top of her head—or maybe it was her legs.

Betty used her position to criticize and bash my entire audit process. Since she was ultimately responsible for the work performed by her office, she had a legitimate interest in how the analysis would be conducted, albeit a limited one. She somehow assumed she had the final say, which she didn't, but I couldn't get anyone in authority to tell her otherwise. They sat silent while she continued to wail, and Rodney continued to swoon. I could not believe it. She was trying to butcher my firstborn, and no one was raising a hand to stop her. I wanted to strangle her, and I found myself mentally weighing the pros and cons of capital punishment. But before I could act on my inclination, the day ended without anything being resolved.

It was then that I realized the hopelessness of the situation. I knew it would be useless to arrange another training session because Betty and her legs would again show up, and the whole thing would turn into a mass argument. That was how she operated. She hated everything she had not developed herself. And since she never did anything herself, she hated everything. At that time, she hated me and my audit more than anything, and I was not too fond of her either.

I then relented and tried to conduct most of the audit myself. For the things I could not do alone, I met individually with a few of my colleagues, and I taught them all they needed to know. The only problem was that a number of the audited welfare cases were located in areas of Betty's domain, so we still had to deal with her on a limited basis. Realizing that I had slipped one by her and that she could not destroy the entire audit, she concentrated on one aspect of it. Sharpening her spiked heels, she attacked it with vigor and gusto.

I already stated that the audit's objective was to determine whether the clients were receiving their restored food stamp benefits, but there was a little more to it than that. The clients were only eligible for restored food stamp benefits if the mistakes were the fault of the welfare office. If the clients themselves caused the problem, they were not entitled to make-up benefits. Also, the benefits had to be restored in the correct amounts for the relevant periods, and everything had to be properly recorded in the case record. Additionally, the clients had to be informed of everything in writing. Our audit process examined all aspects, but primarily focused on whether food stamp benefits were restored when appropriate. The rest of the issues were secondary to that.

Betty was in an especially foul mood that day. Perhaps the store had run out of her favorite brand of pantyhose. (She sometimes wore the kind with the black seam up the back that would drive Rodney absolutely crazy.) I do not know what riled her that day, but she got it into her head that our assessment could not reprimand the local welfare offices when they failed to provide make-up food stamps to the clients who were eligible for them. She claimed that no federal or state regulation had established a time limit for returning benefits to the qualified clients. Instances where the clients had not been reissued their food stamp benefits only meant that the welfare offices had not yet done it.

Had not yet done it? Had not yet done it? I was fit to be tied. We found instances where the offices had been aware of the issue for five years but had not reissued the benefits. In my book, that means they had not yet done it, and they had no intention of ever doing it. Had not yet done it? What was she trying to pull?

Well, she managed to do it. Along with her continuing success in causing Rodney to swoon, Betty succeeded in thoroughly destroying the integrity of the audit. She also quelled my desire ever again to become involved in a headquarters project. As she had done in my training session, she ranted, raved, and disrupted everything with impunity. Those in charge took no action to stop her or correct her behavior. They had never done so in the past, and it became apparent they had no intention of doing it this time either. They felt that, since she had not been able to derail the entire audit as she had wanted, they would make this one small concession to her and maybe, just maybe, she would shut up. And surprisingly, she did—and eventually so did I.

I tried unsuccessfully to persuade the bureau director and anyone else who would listen that if we accepted Betty's demand to ignore situations where the welfare offices had not issued restored food stamp benefits, we would have nothing to report to the Feds. The rest would become irrelevant and inconsequential—nothing at all, really. We might as well report on the conditions of Betty's legs! But my arguments fell on deaf ears, so numbed from Betty's incessant chattering that they could not have heard me even if they had wanted to. But it did not matter because they did not want to. As with everything else in the Elephants' Graveyard, doing nothing seemed to be the preferred solution.

And that is what we did—nothing. Then, when it came time to report to the Feds, we did exactly as I had suggested: we reported on the condition of Betty's legs. The federal government had asked us to investigate and determine if food stamp benefits were being restored to the clients when it was appropriate to do so, but we instead informed them of the moisturizing lotion used by Betty on her legs, the almost imperceptible mole behind her right knee, the circumference of her left calf, and whether or not she preferred an electric or safety razor to keep them smooth and silky. And you know what? No one noticed the difference.

In the Elephants' Graveyard, you will occasionally undergo special audits by elite teams of investigators or other employees of the Department of Public Welfare. You actually have nothing to fear because, most of the time, they are investigating the actions of the department itself and not you. Their primary focus is to determine if you have received everything to which you are entitled. And if they think that you are not getting your due, they usually initiate action to ensure that you get more. So in that respect, you are both on the same side—your side.

Typically, however, their activities amount to nothing more than wasting a lot of time and energy on things that go nowhere to accomplish nothing. So feel free to talk to them if they call or decide to stop by. You probably have nothing to lose by giving them a little of your time. Tell them what they want to know with the full realization that nothing will probably come of it—good, bad, or otherwise. But if you are feeling a little playful that day and want to get a rise out of them, don't answer their stupid, tiresome questions, but, instead, give them an update on Betty's legs. Oh, those legs!

30 THE WELFARE ADMINISTRATOR

WHO IS AL SCHWARTZ?

I continued to advance through the ranks of the Elephants' Graveyard, and one day I was summoned to the state capital to attend a meeting of managers from several of the bureaus in the Department of Public Welfare. There were only about twenty to thirty of us in attendance, and we fit comfortably into a conference room of a training facility just outside the Capitol complex.

As one of the first orders of business, a high-level administrator addressed our group to announce the implementation of a new initiative, one that would affect all of us. She knew it would not be well received, so she tried to forestall any objections by commenting brusquely at the beginning of her announcement, stating that the directive had "come down from above." Immediately, one of the meeting attendees—someone who was never known to remain quiet in these types of situations—said in a conversational tone, one just loud enough for everyone to hear, "Yeah, Auschwitz also came down from above, and we know how that turned out!"

The administrator unsuccessfully tried to hide her displeasure while giving a negative wave of her hand and remarking, "I don't even know who that is." She then proceeded to explain the specifics of the initiative. Stunned beyond all belief, we all turned and stared silently at each other. When the meeting concluded at noon, I made a stop in the men's room before escaping the capital. There, stuck to the bathroom mirror with masking tape, I spotted a piece of lined notepad paper containing the handwritten question, "Who is Al Schwartz?"

The journey from the state capital back to my office was about four hours, so I decided to make a pit stop along the way at another government building about two hours from the state capital, where I had once worked. Before long, I found myself sitting in a tastefully decorated office. For a government office, it was quite comfortable, a far cry from what I had been forced to endure earlier in my civil service career. Back then, the furniture was all surplus stock from the 1930s and 1940s, which had been stockpiled in a warehouse somewhere in the state capital. It was easily requisitioned when needed, and it was always delivered by inmates of the state correctional institutions. Most of the time, the stuff was not worth having and not worth the time it took to fill out a requisition order. For my own part, I made do with cardboard boxes.

However, somewhere along the way, the state began allocating more money to the offices and their furnishings. By the time I had advanced to a level where I was responsible for directing one of the regional offices, the accommodations and furniture had become quite comfortable. That was true of the office in which I found myself, the private office of a man for whom I had once worked. It was my first time back after leaving to take another job in a different city, a job that had eventually led to my becoming the regional office director. I sat across the desk from my friend and former boss.

We discussed the meeting I had attended at the state capital earlier in the day and the various topics that had been addressed. I told him about Al Schwartz, and he almost wet himself. Once he regained his composure, I continued relating what had been discussed at the meeting, and I casually mentioned something a bureau director of questionable competence had said. At the sound of the bureau director's name, my former colleague reacted as if someone had electrified his seat. He jumped to attention and leaned forward on his desk. As his elbows hit the wooden desktop, he pierced the air with his right index finger while proclaiming loudly, "That woman is a dope, a D-O-P-E dope!"

You need to understand that my former boss is an incredibly funny person and a talented pantomime artist. Something like this never failed to propel him into a whole ad-libbed comedy routine. So, after his "D-O-P-E dope" proclamation, he immediately launched into a pantomimed impersonation of the bureau director, which was so true and right on the mark that I was mesmerized. Admittedly, the bureau director under attack was a comical figure with noticeable quirks, but I was in total awe of my friend's ability to mimic her facial expressions so accurately.

I allowed him to complete his standup routine, and when I thought he had concluded, I continued with my report of the meeting. Unfortunately, my next sentence referenced the deputy secretary's response to the comment made by the besmirched bureau director. Once again, my friend's body stiffened before contorting at the mention of the deputy secretary's name. He again silenced me with his antics as he leaned farther across the desk with his index finger pointing directly at my head. "And that woman," he said. "That woman is a bigger dope!" At that point, I knew it was useless to continue with any serious discussion of the meeting, so I sat back and enjoyed the show.

I later learned that his "dope" comments to me were not

the first time he had made them about these two individuals. He regularly referred to one or the other as a "dope in dope's clothing." I must admit that I agreed with his assessment of the bureau director and the deputy secretary. However, I was willing to take it a step further and extend it to include all bureau directors and most administrators in the Elephants' Graveyard, up to and including the secretary of welfare. They were all dopes or, put more explicitly, dopes in dopes' clothing. I also did more than just pontificate about it to someone sitting across the desk from me. I made a concerted effort to disclose this truth to the governor.

He was not just the governor but the "new governor" — the governor-elect, to be more precise. And he was not just the governor-elect, he was the Republican governor-elect, and he had a no-nonsense reputation. He also lived in the city where I worked, and he was just what I had been waiting for. Election Day had been on Tuesday, and following some formalities at the Capitol building on Wednesday, he returned to his home on Thursday for a victory celebration over the weekend. What greeted him in his home mailbox that Thursday morning was a letter from me.

My written message was clear and unambiguous. In the letter, I unearthed all the skeletons and exposed the extent of the problems plaguing the Elephants' Graveyard, all stemming from the incompetence of the senior management staff and the administration officials. His reputation preceded him from his time as attorney general, and the expectations were high for him. It was believed by many that he would take the necessary steps to enact fundamental changes, leading to significant improvements in the system. This was house-cleaning time, and it was his one chance to throw out all the dead wood and make room for new people, new ideas, and new policies. I felt I could provide him with all the ammunition he needed to get the ball rolling. I even advised him to get rid of me! The dopes needed to be shown the door, and it couldn't happen to a nicer bunch of people. There was a new sheriff in town, and heads were sure to roll.

After my initial contact with him, I sat back to watch the carnage ensue. I waited. And I waited some more. And I waited even more. Nothing. Then I started to panic. This was his one shot. If he didn't act now, he would never be able to do it. What was he waiting for? I had gone the route of directly contacting him at his home to avoid the hassles of trying to go through the "proper channels." I did not hide who I was or what position I held in the Elephants' Graveyard. Still, I received no word, and I saw the dopes sitting serenely in their offices, totally oblivious to their imminent demise. There was only one thing I could do: I had to take another stab at it.

I followed up with more correspondence to the governor-elect at his home, but I also branched off in other directions. I contacted the head of his transition team and wrote to various transition team members in charge of the respective committees impacting my department. Many of those people were also elected representatives, all members of the majority Republican Party in both houses. More time passed, but I received no response from them or the governor. I also detected no signs of impending action. Eventually, Inauguration Day came and went, but all remained quiet. Months passed with the status quo unchanged and all the dopes still in charge. Then, one day, the long-anticipated sweeping changes occurred, and I was left dazed and confused.

I cannot remember where I was when I heard the news. All I recall is the feeling in my intestinal tract. The news was swift, and the action was decisive. The dopes had all been promoted! I was utterly speechless. Who was the dope now? I had done everything humanly possible to expose the utter incompetence that infested the higher echelons of the

Elephants' Graveyard, but, in the end, it only resulted in the dopes receiving more power to create even more havoc in the system.

And to make matters worse, the dopes eventually learned about my contact with the governor and how I had referred to them as dopes. Not only that, they knew that I knew that they knew. But they also knew that anyone crazy enough to contact the governor at his weekend home was someone to be reckoned with. If nothing else, the dopes understood the trouble I was capable of causing if they decided to confront me, so they played it safe and just let me be. However, from that time forward, there was always an unspoken tension that pervaded our interactions.

If you are a traveler in the Elephant's Graveyard and you worry because you hear a president or a governor tout the competence and qualifications of a newly-appointed or newly-promoted welfare administrator who is supposed to make the bureaucracy more efficient and accountable, I offer you this bit of advice: fear not. There is a passage in the Bible where Christ says, "Fear is useless; what is needed is faith." But, in the Elephants' Graveyard, not only is fear useless, but so is everything else, including faith. And the most useless thing out there is the welfare administrator. You need to keep in mind that, despite their titles, they are all a bunch of dopes in dopes' clothing. And regardless of how they puff themselves up and what they say, they do not have the slightest clue how to effect any positive change—or at least any change that will negatively affect you in the long run—even when it is spelled out and handed to them on a silver platter. And if you doubt me, you need only ask yourself this question: "Who is Al Schwartz?"

31 YOUR LEGAL PROTECTIONS

HERE COMES THE JUDGE

Hear ye, hear ye, hear ye! The court of public opinion is now in session! Well, not exactly. Fortunately for you, the court of public opinion carries no weight in the Elephants' Graveyard. Everything that takes place there runs inherently counter to the court of public opinion. The public incessantly complains about everything welfare-related, but no one is willing to do anything about it other than complain, so you are safe. The court that requires your attention, however, is the one that has jurisdiction over the Elephants' Graveyard, the one that determines if you will stay on the gravy train should you accidentally (or intentionally) step over the line.

We hear a lot about the judicial system in this country—mainly the criminal and civil courts—and most people have a pretty decent grasp of how the whole system works. They are familiar with prosecutors, defendants, judges, witnesses, and others involved in criminal proceedings, and many people also know how to file a lawsuit against anyone who has wronged them for any reason. Much of this knowledge comes from television, where there are a plethora of commercials by ambulance-chasing attorneys and a whole slew of daytime courtroom reality shows where people air their dirty laundry. I would venture to guess that the inhabitants of the Elephants' Graveyard are far more experienced than others in the intricacies of the legal system, having been criminal suspects and witnesses more often than those in the general population. They are also far more likely to have filed lawsuits, and they have much more free time to watch daytime court shows than those who are out earning a living. But the one area of jurisprudence about which most people plead ignorance is the one governed by administrative law.

The ever-expanding bureaucracy in this country could overwhelm the judicial system in a matter of seconds if all the grievances emanating from it were required to be adjudicated in the regular court system. For that reason, the bureaucracy has been allowed to develop its own court system of administrative law, dubbed a "quasi-judicial system," that has all the trappings of the regular court system. Instead of juries, decisions are handed down by "impartial third parties" acting in the role of administrative law judges, or ALJs. People generally represent themselves at these proceedings, but attorneys often participate. They plead their case to an ALJ much the same way they would plead it before a district magistrate. Everything is conducted like a regular courtroom with oaths, testimony, cross-examinations, evidence, and the like. It is a less formal setting, yet it is conducted with all the grand spectacle of the standard judicial system. Many states have one organization or agency that conducts the administrative appeal hearings for all the state departments. In contrast, other states allow each department to maintain its own administrative court system. I had the opportunity to serve as an ALJ for several years, adjudicating appeal hearings for several state departments, but mostly the Elephants' Graveyard.

As an administrative law judge, I was the final stop in the appeal process for disputes or violations of rules or laws related to welfare entitlement administration. By the time it got to me, all possible attempts for a settlement were deemed to have been exhausted without satisfaction. It was then left to me to make the final, definitive decision and issue a ruling that would be binding on all parties involved. Somehow, it never seemed to work that way.

I had not been on the job long before I started noticing a trend. It seemed that the required pre-hearing attempts at conflict resolution were never initiated, and the preliminary discussions by the opposing parties regarding any of the issues under appeal took place for the first time in my presence. That meant that I would end up with screaming welfare clients on one side of the room, who never failed to bring along their cousin Zeke, a man who had watched too many afternoon court shows and would continually interrupt me with trivial objections. On the other side of the room, I would have welfare caseworkers, supervisors, and managers who had long since stopped performing any of their job functions. Their presence in my courtroom that day was just them going through the motions. Despite my job title, I found myself to be no more than a babysitter or referee in the middle of other people's arguments—stupid, meaningless arguments that they should have been able to resolve themselves in about two minutes.

Then it dawned on me: I was the only one taking this thing seriously. It was a scam being perpetrated by both sides. The representatives from the welfare office (mainly caseworkers and supervisors), being averse or unable to do their jobs because of all the other meaningless welfare nonsense, knew that I would take it upon myself to figure out the problem and work out a solution if they just did nothing. Also, the requirement that they appear at the hearing always earned them a free day out of the office. It was a win-win situation for them, no matter what.

As for the welfare clients, their appearance in my courtroom was always a winning situation (at least temporarily) because their entitlement benefits continued unchanged whenever they filed a timely appeal. And because there were so many appeals and it took so long to schedule all the hearings, the clients could die of old age before they ever got their day in court. Also, it allowed them to tell off their "asshole caseworker" in front of someone—namely me—who they incorrectly assumed wielded some power in the government.

I watched this farce play out day after day until I had had enough. Then, I stopped playing their game, although I respected the game played by each party. The scam was brilliantly conceived and well executed while it lasted. I then became the "hanging judge," which put an end to it. Instead of falling prey to their scam, I started throwing the cases back and telling them to start over and report back to me. This "do-over" especially annoyed the caseworkers because it required them to do their jobs. It also annoyed the clients because, not only had I thrown their cousin Zeke out of my courtroom, I was now forcing them to deal with their caseworkers (instead of me), whom they had just called assholes and who were now extremely angry and determined to screw the clients by enforcing the letter of the law.

I cannot claim my actions made any improvement in the Elephants' Graveyard because I was just one person, but they made my days less stressful and a little more bearable. There were plenty more ALJs out there who were willing to play the game I had ultimately rejected. But as a resident of the Elephants' Graveyard, you cannot let my discernment of the stalling tactics used by welfare recipients via the appeal process stop you from using them to your benefit. By all means, you should attempt them, and you should do so with zeal and vigor.

Appeal everything, even when you know you are wrong

and feel that you will eventually lose. I would even tell you to appeal the fact that the sun rises and sets if you think you can get away with it. The additional welfare time and benefits you receive leading up to the hearing are well worth it, especially if you end up losing your appeal. And by all means, bring your cousin Zeke. His theatrics at the proceedings and the distractions they cause may help to delay the ALJ's decision even longer. You need to understand that appealing an action taken against you in your quest to obtain more welfare entitlements is your constitutional right, the right to due process under the law, and you should exercise that right with abandon. The only suggestion I would make is that you avoid calling your caseworker an asshole at the hearing. Doing so could cause him to initiate even more negative action against you. But then, you could always appeal that, too.

32 FTI

FEDERAL TAX IDIOTS

Fear is a terrible thing. I already mentioned the Bible passage that says, "Fear is useless; what is needed is faith." But if you were to sum up in one word the whole of the Elephants' Graveyard, that word would be "fear": fear on the part of the welfare recipients that their benefits might be terminated; fear on the part of the caseworkers that they will have to waste time learning and implementing some new, inane program that is doomed to failure from the start; fear on the part of the welfare administrators that their incompetence will be exposed and the public will realize that the entire welfare system is a colossal waste of taxpayers' money. But the one overriding fear that grips all welfare workers and administrators, a fear that gets passed along to the welfare recipients as well, is fear of the federal government. I must say that I have never understood that fear.

It is no secret that I hate the federal government. No, I loathe the federal government. I probably could come up with a few more ways to express my contempt for it, but one word I would not use to describe my relationship with the federal government is fear. Throughout my career in the Department of Public Welfare, I never hesitated to speak or act because I harbored fear of what the Feds would think about it. And that fact alone distinguished me from the rest of the inhabitants of the Elephants' Graveyard. It seemed that everyone else in the department thought or acted in a way to avoid running afoul of the Feds. Even when there was no reason to believe the federal government would object to what we were doing, people would head for the tall grass at the mere mention of any federal department, agency, or bureau.

I always considered myself a state employee answerable to the citizens of my state. Instead of kowtowing to federal bureaucrats, I would regularly taunt them. They did not fund my paycheck, so my attitude was, "Screw 'em." Most federal bureaucrats were pompous imbeciles who had a false sense of superiority propped up entirely by the fact that all my colleagues were scared to death of them. But not me. I continually attempted—though unsuccessfully—to persuade others to tell the Feds to kiss off whenever their inherent stupidity ran counter to what we were trying to accomplish. One such area of conflict involved FTI, an acronym for "federal tax information."

No word in the federal lexicon is so overused, abused, or misrepresented as the word "privacy." Attach that word to another hallowed concept, such as federal tax information, and you create the Holy Grail of a non-issue that is prime fodder for governmental exploitation by a federal regulatory agency. And let there be no doubt that the federal government has taken this issue and run with it, leaving behind a wide swath of confusion and fear.

One of the methods the states employ to combat welfare fraud is the use of what is termed the "data exchange." Unlike the early days of welfare, agencies can now exchange identifying client information, such as names, birthdates, and Social Security numbers, to identify individuals receiving benefits from multiple agencies or states. Often, there is no problem with people receiving services from several different agencies, but no one is permitted to receive welfare payments from multiple states, not simultaneously.

The federal government also participates in these data exchanges by providing Social Security Administration and the Internal Revenue Service (IRS) information about individuals who are receiving welfare. The states can then check the welfare records to ensure that the caseworkers know about any income listed on Social Security records and federal W2 and 1099 forms. It is the IRS information, however, that most concerns the Feds when it comes to FTI. Although they are freely sharing federal tax information with the states, they somehow want to keep it a secret that they are doing so, and they require state agencies to jump through a multitude of phony hoops and act out a series of charades that make it appear as if the Feds are not providing this information. It is a totally bizarre and deceptive farce in which I refused to play a part.

When people apply for welfare benefits, they must report their bank accounts and other assets, and caseworkers regularly verify the balances by sending requests to banks and other financial institutions. These requests are completed on official government forms, explicitly designed for that purpose, on which is recorded the identifying client account information. There are also places on the forms to write the bank's name and address so it will display through a windowed envelope.

However, if a state learns through a federal data exchange that a bank submitted an IRS-1099 form for investment income paid to a welfare recipient who failed to report it to the welfare department, the caseworker investigating the issue is not allowed to reveal to the bank where he got the information. When writing to the bank, he cannot even include the account information on the form or fill in the bank's name and address so it can display through the windowed envelope. Instead, he must use a regular envelope and write the bank's name and address on the outside. The form inside the envelope can only contain the client's name, address, and Social Security number—no bank name or account number can be listed, leaving the banks pretty much in the dark. Then, the caseworker must wait, hope, and pray that the bank figures out what is going on and provides the relevant information.

Just being able to access the federal tax information proves equally troublesome. It is permissible to view this information on computer screens, but no one is permitted to print it. And even though the information cannot be printed, offices must have a whole structure in place for storing, transporting, and destroying printed FTI material that is never printed in the first place. Not only that, but there must be a complete hierarchy of positions in place—FTI managers, FTI coordinators, FTI monitors, and FTI investigators—to control and manage the entire FTI security process.

In my office, I posted a blank piece of paper on the wall beside the shredder, labeling it *FTI Destruction Log*. It was there for those imaginary situations when someone in my office would print and then have to destroy FTI material. But since no one ever printed FTI material, the log was blank. I had five similar blank logs from the past five years stored in a locked cabinet (labeled FTI Security Cabinet) to present to the FTI investigators during their office inspections.

I subscribed to the doctrine that said: *If you are that concerned about this information and will not even acknowledge that it exists, then stop providing it to us in the first place; but if you are going to give it to us, then own up to it and get off our backs.* As I said before, I refused to participate in their little charade. Even when I was an administrative law judge, I would regularly dismiss cases that hinged on an FTI exchange, where the caseworker was afraid to enter it into evidence for fear of exposing the FTI charade. Whether as a caseworker, examiner, judge, or manager, I never succeeded in getting anyone to break ranks and accept my premise that the data exchange was just another tool for doing our jobs and the Feds be damned. Everyone was just too afraid of violating the sacred "privacy" privilege bestowed on federal tax information.

If you find yourself cornered or on the verge of being exposed as a welfare shakedown artist, simply scream at the top of your lungs that your privacy has been violated due to improper sharing of federal tax information. Never mind that you don't pay any federal taxes and wouldn't know a tax return if it came up and bit you on the ass. The welfare dopes with whom you are dealing are incapable of figuring that out, so you are home free. Besides, their paralyzing fear of the federal government over this issue makes any rational thought on their part impossible. They will leave you alone as they run to the shelter of their blank FTI destruction logs, hoping the Feds don't question them about anything. In the meantime, you are free to carry on as you damn well please.

33 CORRECTIVE ACTION

BAD ANGELS

Sister Margaret Mary Alacoque was my second-grade teacher. My mother always said how young and pretty she looked, but in her religious habit with its flowing black veils, I couldn't tell. To me, she was merely large, black, and foreboding. Thinking back now, I suppose she was young, at least younger than the other nuns. Youth, however, is a moot issue with nuns; they all seem ageless. But that's beside the point. All I am trying to say is that Sister Margaret Mary Alacoque was my second-grade teacher, and I have come to believe that she knew what I would become in my professional life.

The Catholic school I attended did not use letter grades for evaluating performance in the first and second grades, but Sister Alacoque had her own way of letting us know what was satisfactory and what was not. Her system was based on a series of three rubber stamps, each one bearing the likeness of an angel. One angel was bright and cheery. Its halo sparkled, and its smile beamed. It spoke some congratulatory message about heavenly work. To find this stamp imprinted on a test or a returned homework assignment meant everything, and most of my classmates would rush home with it in hand to show their proud parents.

Another stamp bore the likeness of an angel who was still smiling, but its smile was not as glowing as its colleague's. Its wings and halo were not as neat and trim, but it was still a good angel, appearing reasonably happy. Its comments on the exam or homework assignment were commendable, but the knowing look in its eye made it clear that there was plenty of room for improvement. Upon finding this angel stamped on their papers, my schoolmates would also rush home to show their slightly less proud—but proud nonetheless—parents.

And lastly, there were the bad angels. Lucifer and his followers were bad angels, and second-graders in Catholic school knew darn well what happened to them. Therefore, you can imagine how we felt when an exam or homework assignment was returned to us with one of these babies stamped onto it. Although my recollection is a little hazy when I try to visualize the other two angels, a clear image of the bad angel is still imprinted in my memory. Stamped with red ink instead of black, the bad angel had drooping wings and a pitiful halo. You could not see its face because its hands were covering it. And printed neatly beneath the image was the declaration, "This is so bad I can't bear to look!" Needless to say, not many of these found their way into the hands of parents, proud or otherwise.

I was never one to take any of my graded papers home to my parents, regardless of whether they were good, bad, or indifferent. Somehow, even back then, they never meant much to me. Therefore, I let them accumulate inside my desk throughout the year, that is, until the day Sister Margaret Mary Alacoque walked behind my desk and caught sight of it bursting at the seams and set to explode from all the papers packed into it. She then proceeded to make an example of me in front of the class by pulling out each paper separately and commenting on it while I stood mortified beside my desk. The tremendous embarrassment of that event scarred me, and the memory of it haunts me to this day. My writing about it now attests to that fact.

In the end, I survived Sister Margaret Mary Alacoque's verbal assaults, and I grudgingly agreed to take all the papers home to my parents that night. I would have agreed to anything at that point just to put an end to the uncomfortable scene. If my memory serves me right, I think I threw all the papers into a trash can on my way home, and my parents never did get to see them. Sister Margaret Mary Alacoque's angels—and grades in general—never meant much to me.

I never knew what became of Sister Margaret Mary Alacoque, but I speculate that she somehow became involved with the Elephants' Graveyard. I say that because of all the introspection that is mandated in the welfare department under the guise of "corrective action." Roaming the backcountry of the Elephants' Graveyard are scores and scores of inspectors, investigators, and auditors whose job it is to examine the work of the caseworkers and tell them everything they are doing wrong. Many of these folks are federal employees, while some are state employees. I am sure there are even some county employees performing these functions.

They are sent out and told to identify mistakes, but they usually lack sufficient knowledge of what they are examining to have any positive effect. If anything, they create more work, which leads to even more mistakes. Their lack of any authoritative knowledge of welfare leads them to focus on relatively minor things—petty, inconsequential things. What they mainly find are record-keeping omissions and typographical errors that they use to embarrass the states by standing them up before the federal government and exposing all the papers they neglected to take home to their parents. It is a sure sign that the inspectors are around when you start finding Sister Alacoque's angels stamped in the case records.

Standing before the federal government and having all your bad angels exposed is terribly traumatic for the states because they know the Feds stand poised and ready to slap them with financial penalties, so they will promise anything to end the uncomfortable scene and avoid the federal money sanctions. They achieve this by promising corrective action, specifically by creating plans to correct the mistakes and prevent their recurrence.

Most of the ills in the Department of Public Welfare are caused by mistakes made by the caseworkers themselves. These mistakes are, for the most part, oversights made by over-stressed individuals who have reached their saturation point for absorbing the myriad of regulations that are supposed to govern their actions and determine the way they disburse the welfare monies. The only corrective action that will remedy these types of mistakes is the simplification of the welfare regulations and policies, along with the hiring of more caseworkers to reduce the number of families for which each caseworker is responsible. But that is not going to happen.

The only option left open to the states is to develop and produce large, grandiose plans that address the identified problems. A typical corrective action plan will divert badly needed welfare funds from those in need to pay for training seminars that re-educate caseworkers on how to place a check mark in a particular box on an obscure form, or it might address the physical restructuring of an entire office's floor plan to ensure that computer screens do not face toward outside windows or open doorways. You may have heard the phrase, "Don't sweat the small stuff." Well, in the Elephants' Graveyard, it's the exact opposite.

Although these corrective action plans might meet the demand of the federal government for evidence that concrete steps are being taken to improve the welfare delivery system, they only exacerbate the problem by pulling the caseworkers away from their actual jobs to respond to all the bad angels Sister Margaret Mary Alacoque's former students are stamping in their case files.

So, how does all this affect you as a resident of the Elephants' Graveyard? Well, it makes your life easier because, as everyone gets bogged down addressing the multitude of frivolous corrective action plans created to deal with the stupid mistakes detected by the auditors, there is no one around to keep an eye on you. So sit back and don't sweat the small stuff; your caseworker and the entire welfare office staff are already doing that for you. And don't forget that Sister Margaret Mary Alacoque's bad angels always had their hands covering their eyes, so even they can't see what you are up to.

34 FOOD STAMP BONUS MONEY

LET'S MAKE A DEAL

It was my first—and last—statewide management conference held at the state capital. Earlier, I mentioned a smaller management meeting I had attended with representatives from just a few bureaus, but this was my first sizeable statewide gathering. The entire management staff of the Department of Public Welfare was brought together at one of the ritzy hotels for a three-day welfare extravaganza: three whole days of exciting and stimulating discussions about all things welfare-related and the many intricacies of the Elephants' Graveyard. I had spent the majority of my career dodging such things, but I was sucked into this one because I was already at the state capital for another meeting I couldn't avoid. Fortunately, I had received approval for vacation leave that was scheduled to begin the afternoon of the first day of the conference, so I only had to attend the activities in the morning.

Much of the morning involved registration, with the attendees arriving and checking into their rooms. Afterward, everyone sauntered into one of the large

179

conference rooms to mingle with the other management participants around a breakfast buffet staffed by hotel employees serving coffee, pastries, and doughnuts. Most of the participants knew each other, and they used the opportunity to catch up on old times and to network with the senior management types in attempts to obtain higher positions in the bureaucracy.

I found that I never had much in common with these people. I knew many of them by sight, but I shared no personal relationship with any of them—it was entirely professional—so I hung back and focused on my beach getaway, which was scheduled to begin in a few hours.

At 10 a.m., everyone was ushered into a large ballroom for the welcoming ceremony. The vinyl chairs were arranged in straight parallel rows that seemed to extend for miles, radiating back from a raised stage. The Department of Public Welfare is the largest department in the state, and it employs a significant number of people. Because it is your typical bureaucracy, it is incredibly top-heavy with a vast number of management employees. When the participants took their seats, the sizable crowd resembled a moving ocean of heads and shoulders as they bobbed, weaved, and turned in conversation while awaiting the signal to quiet down.

The stage contained two large speakers and an enormous projection screen on which ran a slide show, the projector clicking through images of the people and places comprising the Elephants' Graveyard. There was a single podium in the center of the stage to which strode the head of the Bureau of Operations. She raised a finger to her lips to signal that everyone should quiet themselves before identifying herself and stating that she would be emceeing the welcoming ceremonies. A few stragglers continued making their way to their seats with coffee and doughnuts in hand.

Because I had been caught daydreaming about my

vacation plans while standing in the corner of the refreshment room, I, too, was one of the stragglers, preventing me from securing a place in the back. In fact, the only available seats upon my arrival were near the front. To make matters worse, others from my division had planted themselves in the first row, saving a seat for me. As I appeared in the doorway, they began waving frantically while pointing to my reserved chair. The sand and sun of my vacation never seemed farther away than they did at that moment.

Left with no other option, I took my seat in the front row and set my face like flint, hoping to weather the next two hours until I could make my escape. I kept telling myself that it could have been worse, that I could have been forced to stay the entire three days. But then something happened that made me doubt if it actually could have been worse.

The morning session was a welcoming ceremony devoted mainly to the keynote address. I cannot remember what came after that because I was struck so much by the speech that my mind tuned out everything from that moment on. Actually, it was not the keynote address per se; it was just one sentence from the speech that hit me—the first sentence.

The keynote address was delivered by the deputy secretary of welfare. She was a petite woman who crossed the stage to polite applause when introduced by the emceeing bureau director. She placed her notes on the podium as she looked out at the audience and announced that our state had increased the food stamp caseload by some gargantuan amount. In precise timing with her words, the projection screen flashed a graphic that read BONUS MONEY.

My first reaction was, "This is not good." But the audience apparently disagreed with me because everyone— except for me—immediately burst into applause that seemed to drone on endlessly. I remember asking myself,

"Am I the only one not clapping?" I then turned around to witness a syncopation of nodding bobbleheads and a tempest of applauding hands. To my dismay, I confirmed that yes, I was the only one not clapping. My next reaction mirrored my first, "This is not good." Everything said after that was inconsequential, and I totally tuned it out. The first sentence of the address and the applause it elicited were all that mattered then and all I remember of the conference now. Before I knew it, I was in my car driving to the shore, telling myself, "This is not good," while also wondering, "Who were those people?"

So why had everyone been clapping? Very simple: bonus money. Bonus money is a concept that was included in a 1996 law known as the Personal Responsibility and Work Opportunity Reconciliation Act. The name of the bill was too long to use in discussion, so we shortened it to its acronym, PRWORA (pronounced something like "purr-war-a"). Lay people knew it as the Welfare Reform Act, a law that was purported to have changed welfare as we know it. Well, it sure did that. It gave us bonus money.

Bonus money (referred to as "performance bonuses" by the Feds) is gobs and gobs of money—somewhere around fifteen to twenty million dollars—the federal government promises to pay each year to the top few states that can raise their food stamp caseload numbers the most. Rather than refer to it as "increasing the statewide food stamp caseload," the Feds call it "customer service" and "increasing program participation." However, the result is the same: increasing the public's dependence on food stamps and other government assistance.

It amounts to a competition among the states, and they take it seriously. A state can obtain an extra four to five million dollars if it can get itself into the top three or four states that have increased the number of food stamp recipients the most that year. This is big money, and everyone wants a share of it. That is why you now see aggressive advertising campaigns designed to lure people into the Food Stamp Program. It is also why the eligibility requirements for food stamps have almost been eliminated. And it is why some states have begun issuing unsolicited food stamps to people based on the assumption that they probably qualify for them. It does not matter that these people have not requested or applied for food stamps; they receive them anyway until they actively turn them down or send them back.

You could not call this extortion because extortion involves the *taking* of money from someone through intimidation or the abuse of authority. This is the *giving* of money through intimidation and the abuse of authority. I guess it is more bribery than anything else. The Feds bribe the states with bonus money to increase food stamp distribution, and the states, in turn, bribe people with food stamps to help them secure more bonus money. Regardless of what you call it, it works, and it's not likely to change.

If you maintain a mailing address in the Elephants' Graveyard, you can rest assured that your food stamps are not going away anytime soon. If anything, the amounts will continually increase while the eligibility requirements steadily decrease. And if you do not yet have an address in the Elephants' Graveyard, just wait; you'll soon have one. Keep checking your mailbox because stuck somewhere between your Publisher's Sweepstakes envelope and your gas bill could be your unsolicited and undesired food stamp EBT card, which you are obligated to accept and use because it enables your state to qualify for federal performance bonus money that helps keep the population of the Elephants' Graveyard fat, happy, and dependent.

35 SOME PARTING THOUGHTS

GO-GO LAKE

Go-Go Lake was a product of the 1960s, as its name would imply. And like many other outgrowths of the 1960s, it survived and carried over into the 1970s. That is when I first encountered it. Although it lacked the luster and shine of its youthful heyday, it still maintained a loyal following, sustaining itself long enough to allow me the pleasure of experiencing it.

To the best of my knowledge, there existed no written directions to Go-Go Lake—only the vivid recollections of those fortunate enough to have visited the spot served as a reference point and guide to discovering it. However, it was almost impossible to find anyone willing to provide verbal directions. For some reason, that was never done. To go to Go-Go Lake, you had to be taken there by someone who knew the way. Like migrating geese, the oldest and most experienced commanded the lead. Having made the journey more times than the rest, only he could be trusted with the task. Fortunately, there was never any difficulty in finding a guide to lead the way. Be it the first or fortieth time, a trip to

Go-Go Lake was always an adventure.

Go-Go Lake sat on a forsaken back road near the university I was attending. It was the brainchild of an eccentric little man, whom we immortalized with the title *The Creator*, and it consisted of just a few acres of land and two artificial ponds dug out with a large shovel crane. The ponds were fed by an underground spring or some other substitute water source that was not readily apparent. A strip of ground, broad enough to be traversed on foot, separated the two bodies of water. Erected on this narrow strip of land was a diving board extending out over one of the ponds. The structure appeared functional, although I never saw it used. A rickety bridge led to an island situated in the middle of the other pond. This structure never appeared functional and was certainly not used. A physical description of Go-Go Lake, as such, might not seem that unusual, but there was more.

Surrounding the ponds was the most extraordinary collection of tacky paraphernalia imaginable. Stone, clay, and plaster statuettes covered the grounds. Pink flamingos perched in the shallows near the water's edge while rubber ducks floated freely across the surface of the ponds. Penguins, donkeys, and black jockeys holding lanterns stood frozen in suspended animation. Plastic birds and owls were strategically placed high in the trees, keeping watch over the art balls and globes that littered the two or three acres of land, all of them shimmering in a rainbow of colors. Religion even crept into this burial ground with Buddhas and statues of various saints professing their faiths. Wooden Indians, goats, pigs, and replicas of a few dozen other creatures also called Go-Go Lake their home. And to top it off, running helter-skelter amid all these facsimiles of life was one live dog that barked incessantly, barking not at the various inanimate objects inhabiting the grounds but at the living creatures that came to visit this menagerie.

A town sat beyond the ponds at the base of a hill. Well,

not actually a town; it was more the facade of a town, such as a stage prop from a movie set. Of course, it was a western town with a sheriff's office, saloon, and general store. A few of the doorways actually led to enclosed rooms. This proved convenient if you needed a place to change clothes or simply desired some privacy.

As would be expected, Boot Hill sat directly behind the town. A sign conveniently placed there advised you of its identity in case you weren't already aware of it. Tombstones and crosses covered the hillside. They bore the names: John F. Kennedy, Jesse James, Abraham Lincoln, Martin Luther King Jr., Billy the Kid, and a multitude of others. There appeared to be no recognizable standard for determining the choice of names other than being dead. My own personal wish back then was to be buried at Go-Go Lake alongside Abraham Lincoln.

Shade was provided by the many trees scattered across the property, some of them containing nooses with facsimiles of several notorious outlaws occupying a few of them. In addition to exhibiting nooses, bodies, and plastic birds, the trees also announced the Good News of salvation in the form of scriptural passages painted on wooden planks and nailed to the trunks and boughs. But despite all these oddities, it is essential to recognize this one crucial thing: Go-Go Lake was not so much a place as it was an idea.

The Creator lived directly across the road from Go-Go Lake in an average-looking house. He maintained his creation with devoted care, cutting the grass and applying fresh coats of paint whenever needed, and no one ever thought to question why. It became a favorite haunt of the local college students, who delighted in exploring and studying it. For those not into exploration or studies, it also provided an ideal setting for lounging around, drinking beer and wine, and throwing Frisbees—free of charge, of course. None asked why he had created it or what it was supposed to be. They just experienced it, enjoyed it, and accepted it for what it was: Go-Go Lake. It even found its way into the college classrooms, being about the only recognizable example of camp art existing in the area, and the university regularly sponsored field trips to it.

Then, one day, *The Creator* suffered a debilitating accident, leaving him unable to care for his creation or maintain the upkeep of the place. This, however, did not quell the spirit of its loyal following. Go-Go Lake was more a state of mind than freshly painted signs and statues. The students continued to visit and pay homage while Go-Go Lake aged gracefully.

Remarkably, the passage of time did not dull its luster. Even the growth of the grass seemed to restrain itself. Perhaps it was out of reverence for what the place represented; I cannot say for sure. Whatever the reason, it did not overgrow Go-Go Lake's hallowed grounds as would be expected. Even the abandoned crane, frozen in time beside the water, did not appear to rust. It became another befitting addition to the grounds, almost a monument, and it seemed to make a statement as to what the place was and always would be. It was at this point in Go-Go Lake's history that I graduated from college and left the area.

They say you can never go back, return, go home, or something like that. Well, I maintain that you can never leave. Once you have been to the mountain or Go-Go Lake, there you are, and you're never the same. You never actually find your way clear, and no matter where you roam, there is always the possibility of finding yourself right back at your starting point. Somewhere in my life, I must have unknowingly made a U-turn because one day I realized that I was back at Go-Go Lake, and not only was I back, but I had become one of the fixtures instead of a visitor.

None of this had occurred to me until I was preparing to make my final departure from the Elephants' Graveyard. Deep budget cuts had led to reduced compensation, but only the management employees were affected. The clients and the unionized caseworkers were unaware that there was even a budget shortfall. So, after five years of watching my standard of living steadily decrease while the cost-of-living dramatically increased, I decided to leave and earn money elsewhere, maybe even find a line of work better suited to my interests and talents—a novel concept in the Elephants' Graveyard. As I bid my adieus and turned to go, I glanced back over my shoulder, only to be struck for the first time with the shocking revelation that I was back at Go-Go Lake. And not only was I back at Go-Go Lake, I had been there all along. Go-Go Lake was the Elephants' Graveyard. Go-Go Lake *is* the Elephants' Graveyard, but I had been unable to recognize it until that day.

I once saw a movie in which it was implied that victims of suicide are destined to live on in the afterlife as civil servants. That genuinely struck home with me because I had spent most of my life as a civil servant in the bureaucracy of public welfare, working in positions that included caseworker, examiner, supervisor, training specialist, program specialist, administrative law judge, and regional manager. Upon leaving the Elephants' Graveyard, I recalled the movie's assertion, which I found entertaining and probably true. But the more I pondered it, the less humor I found in it. I then began asking—no, not asking—demanding—yes, demanding to know what I had done in life that was so heinous and egregious that it deserved a thirty-two-year sentence in the early purgatory of the Elephants' Graveyard. Well?

Well, I never got an answer, and I probably never will. Perhaps it is unfair even to ask such a question. I will never honestly know why fate chose to steer my course in the direction of the Elephants' Graveyard, but that is where the path led. One thing I know, however, is that while I was there, I gave it my all. And, in return for my time, effort, and hard work, I received volumes and volumes of welfare rules and regulations, oceans of bureaucratic paperwork, welfare clients who hated me, managers and directors who took advantage of me, administrators and lawmakers who ignored me, and one live, barking dog that ran haphazardly amid the chaos—just another glorious day at Go-Go Lake.

So, in closing, I will offer something that was told to me by the man who hired me when I first went to work in the Elephants' Graveyard. He wanted to let me know what I was getting myself into so I would not be too frustrated or upset at what I saw. This is what he said:

> The Department of Public Welfare is like an enormous elephant lumbering along step by step. It moves at its own pace and goes where it wants to go, slowly plodding straight ahead, or veering left or right on a whim. It is ugly and grotesque, and no one likes it. Everyone wants something done about it, but no one can slow it down; it is simply too big. No one can change its course or make it go where it doesn't want to go. And, most assuredly, no one can stop it.

That insight into welfare should be reassuring to all who desire to live with the elephant. Take solace in the knowledge that entitlements will always be there and will continue to grow ad infinitum as the elephant plods ahead. And, by now, you should understand and recognize where the path of the elephant leads. It leads to the Elephants' Graveyard, or Go-Go Lake, or whatever name you wish to call it. And if you spend enough time following the elephant, the place you will inevitably end up and the name you will ultimately call it is *Home Sweet Home*.

36 REVIEW SUMMARY

WELFARE FOR DUMMIES

After reading and attempting to discover all there is to know about your welfare entitlements, where are you now? Do you actually know anything more than you did before? Well, maybe, but then again, maybe not. I understand. Lying around while puffing cigarettes in the warm sunshine of the Elephants' Graveyard as the kids run unsupervised through the neighborhood and Lard Ass erects his tent in your backyard, it can be hard to keep your mind focused and remember all you have just read. Therefore, I've put together a quick review that touches on a few key points from each of the preceding chapters, which I hope will help you in your journey toward that land of shade trees, buffets, spare time, and hammocks.

1. The so-called "social safety net" is actually a national hammock that is found only in the Elephants' Graveyard. But before you take that first step into this strange land and claim your rightful place on the hammock, you need to learn and understand a few

things.

2. Never march into the Elephants' Graveyard and tell them precisely what you want. Instead, ask what you can get as the goodies are constantly changing, and you don't want to miss out on something special just because you specifically asked for something else.

3. Be the loudest or most bothersome resident of the Elephants' Graveyard so that the caseworkers will give you what you want—and a little extra—just to appease you and make you go away.

4. Always view and refer to what you receive as an "entitlement" and not a "benefit." A benefit can be taken away, but an entitlement is yours by right and can never be taken away.

5. Choose a secluded place to live that is not easily accessible to the prying eyes of caseworkers, auditors, and welfare investigators.

6. Make yourself appear as pathetic as possible so the bleeding heart liberal caseworkers will feel obliged to take care of you. Alternatively, if that is not possible, at least cultivate some endearing eccentricity, so they let you stay on the hammock purely for the entertainment value.

7. Fill your days with interests and amusements you find enjoyable, but be careful to avoid things that get you thrown off the hammock, such as learning a skill or trade. If anything, you should seek out activities that extend your stay in the Elephants' Graveyard, such as conceiving new children.

8. Understand the real value of food stamps and

safeguard them as you would any other legal tender. Don't lose them, sell them, or give them away.

9. Having minor children is the safest and surest bet for staying on the national hammock.

10. The best fathers in the Elephants' Graveyard are those who are absent, disabled, or deceased.

11. Medicaid has become so vague, confusing, and all-encompassing that no one understands it anymore. You are bound to find some illness or ailment that allows you to qualify for it.

12. The best strategy for surviving something like workfare involves cooperation and patience because the program always fails and eventually goes away. If you find you are too impatient to wait, you can always try to undermine it while pretending to cooperate, but that can be difficult, as it requires a lot of skill.

13. You may be forced into training programs from time to time, but rarely does your participation lead to employment. It usually only amounts to a temporary inconvenience. Once again, cooperation is the key.

14. Attempting to get a minor child recognized as an adult can sometimes result in more money; however, you first need to determine if it will hurt your eligibility for federally funded cash assistance and if your state provides state-funded cash assistance.

15. Feel confident that, as your children follow in your footsteps, they will receive even more welfare goodies down the line than you did because new entitlements are constantly springing up, and the benefit amounts are continually increasing.

16. Children under a certain age will exempt you from the work registration requirement, so you should always endeavor to have a child in your home under that age.

17. The names of programs and entitlements are constantly changing as policymakers try to mislead the public. But don't be fooled. Realize that all newly-branded programs and entitlements are the same as they were before.

18. Ensure that you stay informed about all the goodies to which you are entitled by gaining access to the Public Assistance Eligibility Manual. However, there is a downside to this in that staying informed requires a significant amount of research and effort.

19. Reports are a fact of life in the Elephants' Graveyard, and you have no choice but to endure them. Be aware, however, that failing to at least feign cooperation with the reporting requirements can set the hammock spinning and leave you flat on your back.

20. The EBT card is the greatest medium ever invented for normalizing the receipt of welfare, so use your card freely and boldly without shame or humiliation.

21. Like it or not, you will have to read all the junk mail you receive from the Elephants' Graveyard, even though you won't understand most of it. You never know when they'll sneak in a compliance notice or send you a letter announcing your expulsion from the hammock.

22. Get to know the people in the Welfare Rights Organization, and run to them anytime you feel aggrieved by your caseworker or anyone else in the

Elephants' Graveyard.

23. Agree to register to vote anytime you are asked, but under no circumstances should you ever vote in a primary or general election.

24. Do your best to learn and understand all the jargon and acronyms used by your caseworker so you will be able to read and know what is going on in your case file.

25. Realize that energy assistance is just another welfare entitlement, but it is significant because it can help you qualify for more goodies in other programs. You should be able to concoct some energy expense justification—regardless of how bizarre—that will qualify you for it.

26. Do not fear registering for work when required to do so, as registration has never secured anyone a job and is unlikely to do so in the future.

27. If you find your case assigned to a caseworker with a nasty attitude or a professional caseworker with a degree in social work, you should change your name or address—depending on whatever the office is using to assign caseloads—to get your case transferred to a less predatory and possibly more eccentric caseworker who will leave you alone.

28. Watch out for the welfare police who are sent out to rout you, but be aware that the administration does not have much of an appetite for this sort of thing, so the efforts of these hired guns will be short-lived.

29. Special auditors are relatively harmless creatures, and they are usually looking into issues larger than you. Their efforts rarely amount to anything, so you

are free to ignore them if you wish.

30. Welfare administrators, although they wield considerable power, are relatively uninformed and lack insight into what is actually happening in the Elephants' Graveyard. They don't pose much of a threat to you.

31. You have a constitutional right to appeal every action that is proposed or taken against you concerning your receipt of welfare, and you should avail yourself of this right at every turn. If nothing else, it will give you more time on the hammock until they figure out what to do with you.

32. Everyone in the Elephant's Graveyard is terrified of being accused of violating privacy rights, especially when connected to federal tax information. So, your defense against any accusation thrown in your direction should always be to allege a violation of your privacy rights concerning federal tax information.

33. State and federal auditors are crawling all over the place, but their targets are generally the caseworkers who must then spend so much time addressing the trivial issues raised by the auditors that they have no time to bother you.

34. The welfare administration, although publicly professing otherwise, is always striving to get you more and more goodies, and it will go to extraordinary lengths to attract more people into the Elephants' Graveyard to fill up the hammocks.

35. They say that home is where the heart is, but you will quickly discover that it is actually in the Elephants' Graveyard, where your hammock is

slung, and they are serving up a hearty portion of "S" suffix soup.

ABOUT THE AUTHOR

Joseph K. Waltenbaugh worked within the public welfare bureaucracy for thirty-two years, starting at the lowest level in a county welfare office and advancing to finish as the director of one of the regional offices in the Bureau of Program Evaluation. He also spent several years adjudicating welfare-related cases as an administrative law judge in the Bureau of Hearings and Appeals. His professional and personal insights into the culture of welfare, gained through interactions with some extraordinarily unique individuals and unusual situations, formed the basis of this book.

Although the majority of his career was spent working in government, he also had outside work experience that included groundskeeper, gravedigger, bartender, power plant laborer, road crew laborer, railroad operator, public school teacher, and small business operations officer. As an author and avid sailor, he now spends his time writing and sailing either on the inland waters around his home or the coastal waters of southwest Florida. His political and creative writing can be viewed at the website www.waltenbaugh.net. He also shares his sailing knowledge and experience on the website www.bananawind.us.

www.ingramcontent.com/pod-product-compliance
Lightning Source LLC
Chambersburg PA
CBHW070353290526
45790CB00004B/1475